SISKIYOU COUNTY LIBRARY

3 3871 00 2268

DISCARD

D0090281

"While Meb's performances have shown me what is possible for American distance running and urged me, his teammate, to press in for more, his overcoming spirit through the lows have shown me what it looks like to be a real man. Meb has the remarkable capacity never to lose hope and to experience joy in his life no matter what his circumstances. He is truly gracious in victory and defeat. It is this characteristic that I admire most in Meb."

RYAN HALL
2008 U.S. Olympic team, marathon; U.S. record holder in half marathon

"Just when there was a need for another American hero in our sport, along came Meb. He epitomizes everything this sports stands for—courage, determination, commitment, and above all, respect. There is no better role model in our sport than Meb Keflezighi."

DAVE MCGILLIVRAY
Race director, BAA Boston Marathon; president, DMSE, Inc.

"No runner has endured a longer or more arduous marathon than Meb Keflezighi—from Eritrea to Italy to the USA—or conquered the distance with as much optimism, resilience, and grace. *Run to Overcome* is the inspiring story of the man who led the rebirth of distance running in the States. A truly American story."

JOHN POWERS
Boston Globe

"I first saw Meb run as a freshman at UCLA, where he immediately made an impact on collegiate distance running. Meb seems to make an impact wherever he goes and on whatever he is involved in. Whether it is inspiring a resurgence in U.S. distance running or helping his family realize the American dream, Meb is an iconic example of a person setting out to be the best that he can be."

RAFER JOHNSON
1960 U.S. Olympic gold medalist, decathalon

"Meb is one of the key figures who has put U.S. distance running back on the map. More important, he is a personal inspiration to so many people. It is not what he has achieved, but how he has achieved it, that is most remarkable. He has overcome incredible adversity and accomplished what many thought was impossible. Through it all, Meb's positive outlook and the importance he places on family serve as an example to us all."

DOUG LOGAN
CEO, USA Track & Field

"Runners and nonrunners alike will be moved by the incredible life story of Meb and the Keflezighi family. Strong family values molded Meb into a determined, humble, and hungry competitor. *Run to Overcome* is his story of triumph, perseverance, and victory. It will move you, not just to run faster, but to go through life with the passion and grace of this truly blessed athlete."

> DEENA KASTOR
> *2004 U.S. Olympic bronze medalist, marathon; U.S. record holder in marathon and half marathon*

"This book is a must-read for every coach and athlete in America. Meb's journey has displayed the true qualities of Olympism as well as any Olympic athlete past or present. It is this magnificent display of values that has propelled him to become one of America's greatest distance runners."

> COACH JOE I. VIGIL
> *U.S. Olympic distance coach, 1988 and 2008*

"*Run to Overcome* provides a fascinating inside look at Meb's efforts to strengthen American distance running."

> BILL RODGERS
> *Winner of multiple New York City and Boston Marathons; former American record holder in the marathon*

"Meb's story is the American dream. He has worked hard to succeed both personally and professionally and to create a better life for his family and those around him. *Run to Overcome* is a book that anyone looking to understand what success really is should read."

> DR. HARVEY SCHILLER
> *CEO, GlobalOptions group; former executive director, U.S. Olympic Committee*

"Meb's vision, passion and disciplined execution have made him an exceptional athlete. While competing with Meb over the years, I had the pleasure of learning that he's even a better human being than he is an athlete. As Meb continues to couple these exceptional talents and traits, there is nothing he can't accomplish."

> BOB KENNEDY
> *1992 and 1996 U.S. Olympic team, 5,000 meters; U.S. record holder in 3,000 meters*

"Meb's family instilled in him a persistence and toughness that allowed him to rise above barriers and setbacks that would have defeated most athletes. Meb made himself into a great runner by working on every aspect of the art and science of running. His dedication to purpose and to the details of training is unsurpassed by all the great athletes I have worked with or observed."

> COACH BOB LARSEN
> *Four-time NCAA Coach of the Year (track and field/cross country); coach, Mammoth Track Club*

"Meb's early years in Eritrea were very similar to mine in Ethiopia. His family's journey ultimately landed him in the United States at a young age. Meb has utilized the support and resources around him to get the most out of his God-given talent and has gone on to become one of the best distance runners in U.S. history. Meb is someone I respect and admire, not only for his achievements but also for his character."

HAILE GEBRSELASSIE
Marathon world record holder

"Meb's story is one of the most compelling I know, and one that will lift all spirits. His victory in New York was much bigger than an individual win—rather, it was a win for a family whose story represents the best of this nation."

MARY WITTENBERG
CEO and president of New York Road Runners

"Meb is a natural runner with a stride as smooth as silk. What I love most about Meb, though, is the way he communicates a message of diversity, so that runners of all races, colors, and abilities are accepted and celebrated in the great sport of running."

BART YASSO
Chief Running Officer, Runner's World

"Meb and I had our shining moment at the 2004 Olympic Games in Athens. Those of us who know Meb, know he is a very giving person who loves interacting with people. In person, via e-mail, and by phone, Meb advises me and my Eritrean teammates on many matters related to running. I was very happy to see him earn an Olympic silver medal and win the New York City Marathon."

ZERSENAY TADESE
First Eritrean Olympic medalist; men's world record holder in the 20K and half marathon

RUN to

THE INSPIRING STORY OF AN AMERICAN

OVERCOME

CHAMPION'S LONG-DISTANCE QUEST TO ACHIEVE A BIG DREAM

MEB KEFLEZIGHI with Dick Patrick

Tyndale House Publishers, Inc., Carol Stream, Illinois

Visit Tyndale's exciting Web site at www.tyndale.com.

TYNDALE and Tyndale's quill logo are registered trademarks of Tyndale House Publishers, Inc.

Run to Overcome: The Inspiring Story of an American Champion's Long-Distance Quest to Achieve a Big Dream

Copyright © 2010 by Meb Keflezighi. All rights reserved.

Cover photograph of race copyright © by Don Emmert/Getty Images. All rights reserved.

Cover photograph of blue banner copyright © by Claudia Uribe/Getty Images. All rights reserved.

Interior photographs of Meb with flags and on Olympic podium used with permission by Victor Sailer.

Interior photograph of three athletes from PowerBar ad by John Segusta.

Photograph of the ING New York City Marathon courtesy of New York Road Runners, owner/organizer of the event. Photo by Ed Haas/New York Road Runners.

Interior photograph of Meb and Bob Larsen courtesy of UCLA Athletics.

Interior photograph of Meb crossing the finish line copyright © Mike Stobe/Getty Images. All rights reserved.

Family portrait copyright © by Brian Ball. All rights reserved.

Interior wedding photographs courtesy of Solophotos Photography by Samuel Gebreyesus.

Interior screen grab of TV appearance © 2009 Worldwide Pants Incorporated. All rights reserved.

All other photographs are from the Keflezighi family collection and used with permission.

Back cover photograph of road copyright © by P_Wei/iStockphoto. All rights reserved.

Designed by Jessie McGrath

Published in association with the literary agency of Legacy, LLC, Winter Park, Florida 32789.

Unless otherwise indicated, all Scripture quotations are taken from the *Holy Bible*, New Living Translation, copyright © 1996, 2004, 2007 by Tyndale House Foundation. Used by permission of Tyndale House Publishers, Inc., Carol Stream, Illinois 60188. All rights reserved.

Scripture quotations marked NIV are taken from the Holy Bible, *New International Version*,® NIV.® Copyright © 1973, 1978, 1984 by Biblica, Inc.™ Used by permission of Zondervan. All rights reserved worldwide. www.zondervan.com.

Library of Congress Cataloging-in-Publication Data

Keflezighi, Meb.
   Run to overcome : the inspiring story of an American champion's long-distance quest to achieve a big dream / Meb Keflezighi with Dick Patrick.
    p. cm.
   Includes bibliographical references.
   ISBN 978-1-4143-3957-3 (hc)
  1. Keflezighi, Meb. 2. Runners (Sports)—United States—Biography. 3. Marathon running—United States—Biography. I. Patrick, Dick. II. Title. III. Title: Inspiring story of an American champion's long-distance quest to achieve a big dream.
   GV1061.15.K397A3 2010
   796.42092—dc22
   [B]   2010036103

Printed in the United States of America

16   15   14   13   12   11   10
7   6   5   4   3   2   1

To my parents Russom and Awetash,
who sacrificed their own lives
to seek better opportunities for their children.

To Amoy Letemichael, who made a lot of this journey possible.

To my brothers and sisters who supported and believed in me.

To my wife Yordanos and our children Sara, Fiyori,
and Yohana . . . you are my motivation.

To my classmates, teammates, teachers, coaches,
and friends, who encouraged and challenged me to get
the best out of myself in every aspect of life.

MEB KEFLEZIGHI

To Angie, Poppy, and Uncle Dege:
Nobody ever had three better parents.

To Jody, Eamonn, and Shea:
Nobody ever had a better wife and kids.

DICK PATRICK

CONTENTS

FOREWORD

BY JOAN BENOIT SAMUELSON

"RUN TO WIN"—Meb Keflezighi's tried and true mantra—doesn't begin to describe a life and a career that have helped escalate advancements in distance running among American men in recent years. In fact, winning through running is only a small part of what winning really means to Meb and his family, who emigrated to the United States of America from Eritrea via an escape route through Italy in 1987.

Run to Overcome is an inspiring account and autobiography of a highly decorated American distance runner and marathoner who has become a warm and giving friend to many of his fellow athletes. Meb is also a global role model for aspiring young runners.

I really got to know Meb at the TD Bank Beach to Beacon 10K in 2007. That was his first appearance there, and I consider it one of the most rewarding highlights I have enjoyed as founder of the race. Watching Meb interact with the young runners in my hometown of Cape Elizabeth, Maine, is something that will not fade from my memory anytime soon. His appreciation and respect for his host family, fellow competitors, and race sponsors resonated with the entire community.

Meb's book is full of wonderful stories related to living the American dream. Challenges and hardships were commonplace in Meb's early years, and they were overcome by strong family faith and beliefs. As a boy, Meb developed a work ethic second to none, which was fostered by his father and supported and practiced by his mother and many siblings. Meb is a man who has a strong sense of self and high moral standards. He knows how one person or family can make a difference in the lives of many.

Being able to call Meb my friend is a true honor. As a distance runner, I know the passion and dedication a successful runner needs in order to achieve goals in the sport. Going the extra mile and serving as a change agent in one's community and sport have led to entirely different examples of success, which warrant accolades in Meb's résumé of accomplishments. Meb's story has given and will continue to give countless immigrants and runners reason and confidence to believe in their dreams while following their hearts.

1.0 / AN AMERICAN DREAM

I RUN A LOT AND PRAY A LOT, but I generally don't ask God for a win. I was breaking precedent at the 2009 New York City Marathon.

Knowing I've worked my hardest in training, I am usually content to see whoever's best on race day win. But on November 1, 2009, I wanted—I prayed—to be the first across the finish line in Manhattan's Central Park.

Waiting for the 26.2-mile race to start, I stood on the Verrazano-Narrows Bridge in the front row of nearly 42,000 runners, braced against the chilly temperatures with my beanie, gloves, and arm warmers. I couldn't help but think of how far I had come—and how much I had overcome—since my childhood days in a war-torn African village.

I was born in Eritrea in East Africa and, after a brief stay in Italy, emigrated with my family to the United States at the age of 12 in 1987. Growing up without electricity or running water in a rural Eritrean village, I didn't see television until we moved to Italy when I was 10. I was so naive that I thought real people were inside the TV set. Now I was about to compete in front of 2 million spectators and a worldwide television audience of 330 million. It was just one of many examples of the incredible arc of my life from the third world to the modern world.

In Eritrea, even when I was lucky enough to attend school, I never owned a textbook. Now all my siblings of college age have graduated from or are attending U.S. universities. I went barefoot in Eritrea; now I have a contract with Nike and own enough running shoes to start a small store.

Sometimes I can't believe all that has happened to me. But in New York I really wanted a win and knew it wasn't going to be easy. Race director Mary Wittenberg and elite athlete coordinator David Monti had assembled a strong field, one that Mary was calling the best in race history for men. The lineup included four Olympic medalists and six men who had medaled at the world track & field championships.

Based on PRs (personal records) in the marathon, I was the 10th fastest runner in the field. That seemed like pretty good odds, having only nine faster guys in the race. I've faced a lot worse situations. At the 2004 Athens Olympics, I was 39th fastest on the starting list and wound up with the silver medal. Not many people, other than my longtime coach, Bob Larsen, and I, gave me much of a chance at a medal.

The situation was similar in New York. Some people thought I was too old, at 34, and too complacent, with an Olympic medal, to be a factor. Others assumed my career was in a free fall after a series of disappointments and injuries from late 2007 through 2008 or that I had become too distracted after my wife and I had started a family. The doubters figured I could no longer summon the focus required for world-class training and racing.

What the naysayers failed to consider is that I have been running to overcome all my life. They forgot how driven I am. When I commit to something, I'm all in, all 5 foot 5½ inches and 123 pounds of me. I am often at my best when things look the worst. Maybe it's an inherited ability. My parents are role models in overcoming adversity. It's because of them that my 10 siblings and I are often called the classic American success story.

We came to the United States with virtually nothing but the clothes on our backs and the faith that we were in the Land of Opportunity, where education could be pursued and hard work would be rewarded. I had no idea that running was even a sport when we arrived in the States. My running journey began with a timed mile in my seventh grade phys ed class. I got all my competitive experience in the United States through middle school, high school, and college meets.

Victory at the 2009 New York City Marathon would be sweet for a number of reasons. To begin with, the race hadn't had an American winner since Alberto Salazar won the last of his three consecutive titles in 1982. Second, I had never had a victory in my previous 11 marathon starts, though I had been close at times, including twice in New York. Furthermore, many "experts" thought my career was over, and even I considered retirement in 2008 because of injury. I also wanted to do something special in honor of my friend and former training partner, Ryan Shay, who died of cardiac arrest in 2007 while we were competing in the Olympic trials marathon in Central

Park. Perhaps most important, my parents, wife, and children were at the race. I envisioned accomplishing something special with them in attendance.

So I had plenty of motivation. And who could fail to get inspired by the ING New York City Marathon start venue? It has to be the best in the world. The Verrazano-Narrows Bridge, with its two towers and the upper deck of its two levels filled with runners, is a striking sight.

If you look carefully when the bus takes you to the start, you can see the Statue of Liberty in the harbor. Lady Liberty is a powerful symbol for all Americans, especially an immigrant like me who, while continuing to love my native country, is so grateful for the privilege of U.S. citizenship.

Given my pride in my adopted country, I thought it was appropriate to wear a USA singlet in a race desperate for an American winner. Race administrators and Nike wanted me to wear the singlet to create some buzz among fans. I considered it an honor and a performance enhancer: Spectators would be chanting "USA! USA! USA!" when they saw me, providing an adrenaline boost.

I felt a special relationship with the New York City Marathon. It's where I ran my first marathon in 2002, finishing ninth. I vowed never to run another marathon after that race; now I call the experience my PhD in the event. I placed second in 2004 and third in 2005. I was 20th in 2006, after suffering food poisoning. So I had a long history of ups and downs with the event.

Twenty-six miles, 385 yards is a long way—a lot can go wrong during that span—even when you're used to running up to 135 miles in a week. I had trouble sleeping the night before, awakening at 12:30 a.m. for the first of many times with even more than the usual pre-race jitters.

At the start line, I was in full race mode, clued in to my body and attuned to my opponents. I had one minor worry. I hadn't been able to do my full warm-up of eight to ten strides of 100 meters at race pace; I was only able to get in two. I hoped that wouldn't be a problem in the early going. But there was no more time for apprehension.

The cannon fired. One more quick prayer and we were off.

RUNNER'S TIP
John Wooden used to begin each basketball season at UCLA by teaching his players how to put on socks. I'll start you with the reminder to tie your shoelaces securely. If you're going for a morning run, make sure you have everything ready the night before so you don't lose time trying to locate necessities.

OVERCOMER'S TIP
Once you've committed yourself to something, pace yourself to the finish line.

2.0 / OUT OF ERITREA

MAYBE I WAS DESTINED to be a survivor.

Of the 10 children my mother gave birth to, she remembers my delivery as the toughest. Even though our family lived in Asmara, the capital city of Eritrea, she did not go to a hospital to give birth. This was still the third world.

When I was born at home, my mother did not have the advantage of her mother's presence, since she had recently died, nor my father—who was away on business. During her difficult labor she lost so much blood that she collapsed and thought the two of us were going to die. There were no medical personnel to help; there was no 911 to call. Neighbors who were experienced in births assisted with the delivery.

Forty days later, when I was baptized in the Eritrean Orthodox Church, my mother was still in pain. Though I'm known as Meb, the full name my mother and father gave me is Mebrahtom, which in the Eritrean language Tigrinya means "let there be light." I've been told I'm a light to my family and native country, but the name comes from my mother's desire to grant a wish of Asfaha, the youngest of her three brothers. As a child, he wanted a younger sibling. When their mother asked what he'd call the child, he answered Mebrahtom if the child was a boy.

I might well have been a victim of the 30-year war between Eritrea and Ethiopia. I was born right in the middle of it—on May 5, 1975—when life in Asmara was unstable and dangerous. Life has been violent in the Horn of Africa for a long time. Eritrea, a triangular-shaped country of about 4 million, has been invaded for centuries, in part because of its valuable coastline along the Red Sea. The country was ruled by Italy from 1890 to 1941 and by Great Britain from 1941 to 1952, when the United Nations created an Eritrean-Ethiopian federation. In 1961 Eritrean rebels fired on an Ethiopian police post and the thirty-year war began. A year later, Ethiopian emperor Haile Selassie forcibly annexed the country. The 1961 to 1991 war for independence against Ethiopia, which Eritreans call the "Armed Struggle," resulted in Eritrea's independence being recognized internationally by 1993—but at a terrible cost. More than 150,000 Eritreans died and nearly 500,000 fled to other countries.[1] Most of the Eritreans escaped to nearby Sudan, but some were lucky enough to make it to Europe, North America, or even Australia. This is one reason why Eritreans can be found all over the world, and why I have distant relatives all over the United States and around the world.

My journey and that of my family would be shaped by the war and the desire of my parents—my father, Russom Sebhatu Keflezighi, and mother, Awetash Berhe—to provide an education for their children. Theirs was an arranged marriage, customary in the Eritrean culture. My father was 18 and my mother 5 when they were engaged, not unusual in Eritrea. They married when Awetash was 12; my father's duty was to continue to raise her into her teens. They had their first child, my brother Fitsum, when my mother was in her late teens. My father was a shopkeeper and businessman in Asmara, where my family had a relatively comfortable existence in a country whose residents today have an average annual income of about $200 to $1,100, depending on how the figure is calculated. By any measure, Eritrea is one of the poorest countries in the world. What Eritreans may lack in wealth, they make up for with determination. The government operates with a philosophy of self-reliance and is thus reluctant to accept foreign aid.

By the time of my birth, there was increasing warfare in Asmara between the Ethiopian military and Eritrean troops. At this stage in the war, Asmara was controlled by the Ethiopians, but the two competing Eritrean independence fronts, the Eritrean Liberation Front (ELF) and Eritrean People's Liberation Front (EPLF), were making a push to take control of the capital city and thus the country. Civilians were sometimes casualties. A few months after my birth, Ethiopian bombs and artillery left a vast fire in the city one night. My dad rushed home from work to check on us. Luckily we were safe, but my mother was alarmed. She convinced my father, who provided supplies and raised funds for the Eritrean Liberation Front, that we should leave town and stay in a nearby village, Adi Tselot, about two miles away.

That night, after securing the family in Adi Tselot, my father returned to Asmara to check on our home. He was also worried about his deaf brother, Beyene Sebhatu Keflezighi, and his brother-in-law, Asfaha, and went searching for them in the city, despite being warned by an Eritrean policeman that Ethiopian soldiers were randomly shooting civilians. Both of them were okay, but a cousin with Beyene had been shot in the leg.

While my dad was at home the next day, Ethiopian soldiers knocked on the door. They had been on a rampage in the neighborhood, raiding homes and destroying property. They interrogated my father, first asking if he had any weapons. When he answered no, one of the soldiers yelled, "Kill him! Kill him! You will not find a bigger outlaw."

The soldiers asked where my mother was. "At her brother's wedding," said my father, making up a story. He did not want them to know that a lot of people were fleeing Asmara for nearby Adi Tselot, which might have jeopardized everyone's safety there.

"Kill him, kill him!" repeated one of the soldiers. "He is lying." Fortunately the soldier in charge took control: "We don't take the life of someone who is in his home. If other military come, tell them we already checked you out."

My father requested documentation that he could continue to stay at home without further problems, but the military said they couldn't provide him with anything except advice to open the door immediately and explain he had been cleared if soldiers approached him again. After they left, my father went inside the house, placed a bedsheet on the floor, and tossed all our clothes on it. He loaded the bundle on a donkey and left our home in Asmara for good. That had been too close a call.

Dad returned to Adi Tselot and took my mother and their

children—Fitsum, Aklilu, and me—to his family village of Adi Gombolo about five miles away. Soon my maternal grand-father, who had heard the word from people traveling out of Asmara, came to check on us. He wanted the family to return with him to my mother's home village, Adi Beyani, about 50 miles away, which was more isolated and therefore safer. Adi Beyani and the nearby larger village of Areza were under the control of the ELF at that time.

My dad thought this was a good idea but wanted to stay for a while in Adi Gombolo so he could monitor our home and the store where he worked in Asmara. He told my grand-father, Berhe Mehanzel, to take my mom and us kids with him. He said he would join us later. My mother issued an ultimatum: "Either my husband comes with us, or we're not going." My mother's stance was supported by her father and by my father's relatives in Adi Gombolo. So by bus and by foot we all set out for Adi Beyani, which was home for the next five years or so. I was not yet three months old when we made the trip.

///////////////

The move to the countryside meant a change in lifestyle. My father went from running a store and overseeing inventory to raising crops and herding oxen, cattle, and donkeys, much as he had done as a child. Unlike in Asmara, there was no elec-tricity or running water in our new village.

We lived in a two-room *hidmo* constructed of stone with a roof of beams, plastic sheeting, and branches—all covered by dirt. One room was used for cooking and the other for eat-ing and sleeping; there was an outside area for the livestock,

separated from the living quarters by a fence. We were a growing family with the addition of Bahghi, the answer to my
mother's prayers for a daughter, and another boy, Merhawi.

As in many Eritrean villages, the church was the center
of community life in Adi Beyani. It was definitely the most
ornate building in the village, and a highlight each year was
the annual celebration of the church's founding and naming.
This daylong celebration included a church service, traditional
music and dancing, and special foods prepared just for the
occasion. Relatives from other villages, many of whom we saw
just this one time each year, came to celebrate with us.

From my parents, I learned early about the power and maj-
esty of God. Our reverence for God extends to our church.
We remember God's command to Moses—"Take off your
sandals, for the place where you are standing is holy ground"
(Exodus 3:5, NIV)—and seek to honor the place where we
come to worship him. That explains the many signs of respect
that are part of our faith—such as kissing the church door and
making the sign of the cross (crossing ourselves) when we pass
by the church. These simple acts may appear strange to others,
but to us they are reminders that God is holy and we are not
to take Him or our faith for granted.

Our parents encouraged us to pray not only when we go
to sleep and wake up, but also when we start and finish any
task, whether it is eating a meal or starting a trip out of town.
My parents' strong belief in a mighty God enabled them to
maintain their faith against all odds—and that's another value
they taught their children. We don't give up easily.

Their perseverance was also shaped by the challenging conditions in which they'd lived all their lives. If you've ever seen

Endurance, the movie about (and starring) the great Ethiopian runner Haile Gebrselassie, you have a feel for our childhood. Much of the day was spent doing chores. The boys were in charge of foraging for firewood. We roamed the sparse landscape, looking for trees and leaves to collect. We used a belt that we twisted into a figure eight and wrapped around our ankles to shimmy up trees to scrape bark or grab leaves.

The search for wood consumed us. Because trees were so scarce, the villages had determined territorial boundaries for collecting wood. One time Aklilu and I were caught roaming outside our area. We had to spend a whole day in another village and weren't released until my mother paid a fine, just like posting bail to get someone out of jail. Because wood was in short supply, dung was also a source of fuel. We collected it from the animals, placed it against the fencing that housed the livestock, and used it for fires after it had dried. Even now, if I'm stretching against a tree before or after a run in San Diego or Mammoth Lakes, I'll think, *This would have been great firewood*, or *This would have been great for a house.*

We had to get water from wells or streams and bring it in large containers to our house. We herded the livestock. In the winter when grass was scarce, the older boys would take the livestock well outside the village to grassier areas, far enough away that they had to stay overnight in *dembe* huts. The next morning, a family member would drop off breakfast and lunch. There was definitely a team approach in our life in the village.

It wasn't all work and no play, however. We loved soccer and played with a makeshift ball made using wadded pieces of plastic inserted into a sock that was then sewn with string. We played games similar to kickball, also with homemade balls. The big social event of the day occurred in the evening when neighbors—adults and children—gathered outside someone's home to tell stories, make jokes, and discuss the local news of the day. There is a strong oral tradition in Eritrea and other African cultures, where news and history are shared verbally, unlike in the United States today, where people tend to rely on written news sources.

As far as I could tell, life seemed pretty good. I did receive one unforgettable lesson in discipline when I was about five years old. My mother asked me to perform some chores around the house, but I was defiant and ignored her. My father overheard the exchange and gave me a stern spanking. To this day I thank him for the lesson. His philosophy boiled down to two rules. First, God is watching you 24-7, so do the right thing at all times. Second, respect your mother. "Your mother is special," he told us.

As Fitsum grew older, my father talked to him about attending school, though Fitsum had no desire to go. My father told him, "You don't understand the value of education. Once you do, you will blame me if I don't give you a chance."

My father entered the two oldest children, Fitsum and Aklilu, into the educational lottery. Only one child per family could attend school. (Many villages used such lotteries, but the number of children from each family who could attend school varied from village to village.) Aklilu won the lottery, so he was the first to attend school.

The war continued until 1991, so violence remained a concern. Once boys approached their teen years, they were in danger of being taken by the Ethiopian military for training and eventual service in their army. Fitsum and Aklilu knew that if Ethiopian troops were in the area, they needed to find hiding places behind big boulders or the brush, where there was a lot of cactus. The typical technique to capture youths was to surround a village and then systematically search it. Sometimes the Ethiopian soldiers would show up at a funeral, since all the villagers would be there, and take away the young men.

One time an Ethiopian soldier asked Fitsum how old he was. Wanting to impress the soldier with his knowledge of Amharic, an Ethiopian language, and to appear older than he was, Fitsum inflated his age to 14. Big mistake. "Let's go," the soldier and his comrades told him. "You're old enough." While the soldiers were occupied searching another dwelling in the village, Fitsum ran away and escaped. He was lucky. Running away is normally reason enough to be shot. Most teens who could not leave the country volunteered in the Eritrean independence movement instead of being conscripted into the Ethiopian army.

Fitsum remembers an artillery attack that left villagers dead and wounded. I don't remember combat, but I did see dead bodies, scattered body parts, and injured people. By the time I was six, the violence had increased around Adi Beyani to the extent that my mother felt my father needed to leave the country to save his life. His role with the Eritrean Liberation Front made him vulnerable. She figured it wasn't a question of *if* he would be killed but *when*.

"What profit will it gain the family if they kill you?" my mother said to him. "You have done a good job planting. There is enough food for the winter. If we need money, I can sell the oxen. You have provided. Go now."

My father was distraught. He was especially worried about what his father-in-law would think. At first, it wasn't much: "She is pregnant, and you are leaving? How can you leave her in this situation?" My mother was carrying their sixth child, but she convinced her father that her husband's departure was necessary.

///////////////

On July 1, 1981, my father left Adi Beyani. I have no recollection of the day he left, but Fitsum has vivid memories. His intuition told him that something was wrong. My father explained that he was making a business trip, which he did periodically, to Asmara. "Don't go for long," Fitsum pleaded. My father, a strong man normally in control of his emotions, had to turn away so Fitsum wouldn't see his tears. "A terrible day," my father calls it.

My father left with his father-in-law's blessing, but some people, including members of my mom's own family, thought he was out of our lives for good. My father had a plan to leave the country and eventually reunite the family. He told my mother that the expected child should be named Bemnet if it was a boy and Amina if it was a girl. Both names mean *trust* in the Tigrinya language. They were making a promise to one another. "I will pray, and someday we will all be reunited in a peaceful land," my mother said.

They would both be tested to the limit before we were all together again. My father began a trek of about 225 miles west to the Sudan border that took seven days, meaning he averaged more than a marathon's length a day. His provisions were a bag of barley seeds, a flashlight, matches, a watch, a two-liter canteen, the equivalent of $25, and a specially made stick for protection. The dangers were Ethiopian soldiers; animals such as hyenas and tigers; snakes and scorpions; and robbers. He tells us now that his biggest worry was leaving the family behind, not the dangers of the journey ahead.

My father typically started walking at 5 a.m., stopping at noon to seek shelter against the sun as well as from soldiers and potential robbers. After three hours hiding in the shade or a cave, he'd walk again until 10 p.m. (Even now, at 73, my father keeps up a strong pace when he walks. I've got to hustle to keep up with him whenever we hike in the California mountains.) At some points he got help from villagers who provided food and shelter for the night. It helped that he could speak our native Tigrinya, the major language of Eritrea; Amharic, the major language of Ethiopia; Italian; and English, so he could communicate with almost anyone he encountered. For navigation he relied on directions from locals and his own instinct.

My father was escaping to save his life, but he felt compelled to help others along the way. Three days into his journey, he encountered a villager who, with his young son, was having trouble herding cattle. The villager was impressed with the way my father handled a rogue cow and asked how someone who looked like a city person knew about cows. My father told him of his village upbringing and his recent years in Adi Beyani. As thanks for my father's help, the villager provided him lunch.

His nights were never restful because he had to be on guard against animals and outlaws. He needed the matches to build fires for protection against hyenas, which are nocturnal hunters. "If you stay close to the fire, they'll stay away from you," he said. My father was aware that human predators could be even more deadly. He had a cousin who had been robbed and murdered on the road while bringing grain to a village.

Though the threats didn't deter my father, he had some close calls. Fording the Mereb River, one of the largest in the country, he suddenly faced deep water and a strong current, making it difficult to get across. On the other side, he bumped into an acquaintance, a guide whom people paid to help lead them out of the country. The man was amazed that my father had made it safely, telling him he wasn't taking people across because navigating the river was too dangerous to try just then. The guide wanted my father to accompany his daughter until she made it to the border in Sudan. Though my father always looked to help, he declined in this instance, saying it would be too dangerous; he needed to be unencumbered to travel more quickly and to avoid soldiers and robbers.

Another time when my father was walking in the forest, he instinctively turned and spotted a man with a rifle behind a tree. The man turned away from him. My father had no idea if the man was a hunter or a robber; he was just grateful the man never fired at him, especially when he later heard gunshots. My father attributes his survival to God's protection and divine intervention. To him, it was just further evidence of an all-powerful God.

Once my father reached the border, he avoided refugee camps and made it the 300 miles or so to Khartoum, the capital of Sudan, by hitching rides. Within a month he had found work, using connections of relatives and friends. He began sending us money. Wiring it wasn't an option; he had to entrust funds to other people going into Eritrea.

Meanwhile, my mother was growing concerned in Adi Beyani, mainly because she didn't like the educational system. A few months after my father left, she decided to move the family back to Adi Gombolo, my father's village, where all of us could potentially attend school.

This was not a simple move for a single mother with five kids and another on the way. We traveled the 50 miles on foot and by bus, carrying as many possessions as we could. The trip was my introduction, at age six, to a larger world. During a walk to the nearest town with a bus stop, I saw a car for the first time. I panicked, thinking it was headed right toward us, and ran into the bushes. When we got on the bus, I was disoriented. Standing in the packed vehicle, I had the sensation of staying still while the scenery outside was being moved. Though I had ridden a bus as an infant, this is my first memory of riding in any vehicle.

Our journey came about the time of harvesting season. Soon after we arrived in Adi Gombolo, we needed to return to Adi Beyani to get our crops. Three times while pregnant my mother made the 100-mile round trip journey on foot and by bus to pick up bundles of food and bring them back to Adi Gombolo. A couple of months after giving birth to a boy, whom she named Bemnet as she and my father had agreed, she made two more round trips.

Later my mother made another decision that required a big trip. After we had plowed some fields, she wanted to take two oxen we owned back to Adi Beyani because the grazing in Adi Gombolo was so poor she feared the animals might die. She left my younger sister, brother, and me in the care of my dad's relatives. Then my mother, a newborn Bemnet on her back, with Fitsum and Aklilu along to help, walked the entire 50 miles in two days, guiding the oxen to Adi Beyani, where the animals remained. At least Mom and my brothers got to ride a bus for part of the return trip.

FITSUM KEFLEZIGHI: My mother is an amazing woman. The courage it took to make those decisions was incredible. She was being both the mother and the father of the family. She could have stayed with her dad and brothers. That would have been comfortable, easy. But she said, "That's not what I want for my kids. If you don't get an education, the only thing you can be is a shepherd." It was a tough time.

Fitsum and Aklilu were still in danger of being conscripted by Ethiopian soldiers, so we were always on guard in Adi Gombolo. My brothers had hiding places if we got word soldiers were near. The violence had not ended either, and it was not unusual to hear gunshots.

A few years later a boy of about 10 or 12 carried a container of grain into the village to be ground. On the way home he was playing with what he thought was a toy that he had discovered on the roadside. Unfortunately, it was a land mine, which exploded. We heard the explosion, and people came out to see what had happened. Women cried upon witnessing another innocent victim of the war. I was part of the cleanup crew that collected the body parts so the child could have a proper burial by his family in his village. That was a harsh way for an eight-year-old like me to learn that life is precious. Here was a kid, not much older than me, who was doing an everyday chore yet never made it home. I learned at a young age not to take tomorrow for granted.

For a time Fitsum, Aklilu, and I attended an informal school in the village. Then Fitsum, Aklilu, Bahghi, and I won the lottery to enter school in a neighboring village, Selae Daro.

Bahghi had been so anxious to get in that every time she passed the Orthodox church in the village, she would make the sign of the cross, kiss the wall, and say a silent prayer that she and I would be lottery winners. She promised God she'd pay the equivalent of 25 cents, a decent amount in our economy, for each of us if we got in. She got the money from my mother, who also had to pay 20 Ethiopian *birr* a year in tuition for the four of us. The money was coming from Dad.

Our schools were not like those in the United States. Students were grouped by proficiency, not age. Typically three students shared a book and two students shared a desk. Pencils and paper were scarce. Most lessons were conducted on a blackboard. Memorization of the material on the board was critical. If you didn't know an answer, you could get slapped, either by the teacher or by other students who knew it.

In the mornings, my mother worked a job requiring her to pass rocks hand-to-hand for building walls—tough, physical labor for which she was paid in cooking oil, flour, and sugar—all stamped as USA aid. With the help of neighbors, Bahghi would stay home to take care of the babies, Merhawi and Bemnet, and do household chores until Mom got back around 1 p.m. Then Bahghi would attend school for the afternoon session.

Hunger was a problem because we relied on growing our own crops for food in a region that suffered famines and droughts during the late 1970s through the mid-1980s. Timing the planting to coincide with imminent rainfall was important and difficult. There was no Doppler radar or 10-day forecast to assist in planning. In the villages, people relied on God for help with rain and farming. Whenever we went through a long dry spell, people would go to the church as a group to pray for rain.

At times food was so scarce that I literally ate dirt. I'd dig into the soil until it became dark and moist, putting it in my mouth so I could soak up some of the nutrients my body craved. Even though it sounds strange, it was a means of survival. I was skinny but had a distended stomach. That gave me my nickname, "the kid with the bloated stomach."

Compared to many other families, we managed relatively well because Dad sent us money and clothes. But we knew families who had to leave the village to beg for food in areas not hit so hard by the famine.

Conditions were tough in the third world. Bemnet contracted severe dysentery, but he survived, although 30 other village children died. Bemnet was so ill that some people told my mom she would be better off if Bemnet died. Of all my siblings, Bemnet came closest to death, but there were other close calls. In Adi Beyani, Bahghi was about four when a large boulder that fell off a wall nearly severed her leg and mangled her foot and ankle. Family members carried her piggyback to three different villages seeking help. Finally, she was sent to a hospital administered by the Eritrean Liberation Front. The two months she spent there planted the seed of her becoming a doctor. When I developed a large, painful abscess on my head, Mom took me to Asmara, where medical personnel removed it without a local anesthetic—and who knows if the scalpel was sterilized. It hurt a lot—I still have the scar—and I cried until I was slapped hard on the face. That was my painkiller.

My father had his own concerns while he remained in Khartoum for about a year and a half. His business experience in Asmara enabled him to start off as a shopkeeper. Because his work ethic and attention to detail were so great, he was given the additional responsibility of unloading and keeping the inventory of products. Before long he was earning triple his starting salary. He worked the bureaucracy just as hard. The plan was for him to get to Italy and then send for his wife and children—my father's family had vetoed the idea of us walking to Sudan to join him there.

We had a guardian angel in Letemichael Tewelde, who had been my father's girlfriend once and with whom he had a daughter, Ruth. Though my father (and our entire family) considers both Letemichael and Ruth great blessings, my dad has had to take responsibility for his youthful indiscretion and the possible challenges it created, for Letemichael, Ruth, and his own wife and kids. I think my mother's decision to embrace Letemichael and Ruth (and vice versa) is a great demonstration of the love and forgiveness available in Christ.

Now, while in Sudan, my father got in touch with Letemichael, who had relocated to Italy, and she worked to get him into Milan. Letemichael, whom we call Amoy Letemichael (meaning Aunt Letemichael), and Ruth are heroes to our family. Letemichael is like Mother Teresa, constantly helping others who were in situations like ours. She was there with financial, logistical, and emotional support.

When my father got to Italy in early 1983, he applied the same strategy he had used in Sudan. He was relentless in his work and in prodding immigration officials. He got a job cleaning homes and offices. The company's owner, Dr. Luigi Brindicci, noticed his work ethic. My father has one way of doing things— the right way, with constant, all-out effort. He doesn't believe in shortcuts. Even when he was paid by the hour, he would work as efficiently as possible, but with much care for the details.

Impressed by my father's attitude, Brindicci took an interest in him and gradually learned about our family's situation. He became a benefactor, helping my father prepare the necessary documents to gain residency status, which he needed to bring our family to Italy. Then Dad began investigating options to get us out of Eritrea.

The separation from his wife and children was agony for him. Watching families play together in Italy brought him to tears. *I just want to go to the park with my kids and play soccer,* he thought. *Will I ever see my family again?* He prayed four times a day for our reunion. Amoy Letemichael kept telling him, "If you trust in God, He will get them to you soon."

My father arranged for us to arrive in Italy via Asmara to Addis Ababa to Cairo to Athens, where he would meet us. We would then travel together to Milan. But he needed help in paying for the trip. When my father informed Brindicci of the travel costs, Brindicci gave him a $6,000 gift toward the $8,000 cost. Dad, who provided the rest, calls Brindicci "a kind man, the best man in the world." My father offered to pay Brindicci back, but he said all he wanted in return was to see the kids saved. My dad still corresponds with and sends updates on my family to Brindicci.

The reunion occurred May 8, 1986, in Athens, nearly five years after my father's departure from Eritrea, and it was a dream come true. I didn't remember my father leaving, but I'll never forget seeing him in Athens. I was first through immigration and ran to him. He hugged me and called me Merhawi. I was so small that he confused me with my brother, four years younger than myself. When I said, "No, Mebrahtom," he burst into tears. He was distraught at how frail we all were. "My kids, my kids," he wailed. He couldn't imagine how much worse it must have been for families not receiving the extra income he had supplied to us.

My mother snapped him out of it: "Don't cry about their size, just make sure all six are here." Athens, which would play a role in my future, will always be a special city to me. Our family was reunited, just as my parents had promised each other.

When we got to Italy, we moved in with Amoy Letemichael. You might think there would be tension between my dad's former girlfriend and current wife, but that would be under-estimating Letemichael and Mom. Actually, they became the best of friends. They consider themselves sisters. Ruth is a full-fledged member of our family. Ruth loves that my mother detests terms like *stepdaughter* or *half sister*. Just as Amoy Letemichael is another mother to us, Ruth is a daughter to my mother. Amoy Letemichael's brothers were also instrumental in helping us throughout the journey from Eritrea to the United States—Baba Tekeste in Asmara, Baba Abraham in Addis Ababa, and eventually Baba Rede in San Diego. (*Baba* is a title of respect Eritreans reserve for their elders.)

But it was not easy in Italy, especially since we could not attend school at first. My father was trying to get us to the

United States, where Ruth had recently immigrated, but we were rejected. So we tried Sweden. We left on a flight paid for by Brindicci—minus my father, who had been hospitalized after a car wreck—but we were not accepted into the country upon landing in Stockholm. At this time my mother was pregnant with child number seven, Adhanet. We had to live for about a week in an immigration camp before returning to Italy, where we spent one night in prison. We children were put in a boarding school. At first, Fitsum and Aklilu were separated from the rest of us. Dad talked to the Red Cross, which arranged for all of us kids to be quartered together, though we were schooled separately. The Red Cross paid for our schooling and other necessities during that time.

My father discovered our application for asylum in the United States had been rejected because he was incorrectly listed as having two wives. He provided documentation showing he had married only once. He also started working other avenues, always persisting though it would have been easy for him to give up and stay in Italy. His motivation to leave was to get us to a better educational system. He wanted to expedite everything because he didn't want us to miss out on another school year.

He started working through the Catholic Church and the Red Cross. Ruth, in San Diego with her uncle, Rede Tewelde, became a sponsor to get us into America. But roadblocks kept materializing in my father's efforts with immigration authorities and officers from the two organizations. In October 1987, my father brought us to Rome, where authorities had us traveling in circles from the U.S. Embassy to Catholic Church offices to Red Cross headquarters. With a wife and seven children in tow, my father was fed up with red tape and the runaround. He slammed his hand down on a table in frustration, telling the Red Cross workers that the family had been mistreated during the past eight months and that he had proper documentation to be admitted to the United States. Conveying a similar sense of urgency had helped him get us out of Eritrea.

A week or so later, on October 21, 1987, we were on a plane to San Diego. There was no way then to predict that Fitsum would graduate from the University of California at San Diego with an engineering degree; that Aklilu would go to UC–Santa Barbara, study economics and political science, and get an MBA; that Bahghi, Merhawi, and I would graduate from UCLA, where Bahghi would also go to medical school and Merhawi to law school; that Bemnet would graduate from UC–Santa Cruz; that Adhanet would graduate from Stanford. There would be three more children born in the United States: sister Fnann, now chair of the Black Student Union at UC–San Diego; sister Ziada, who attends UC–Berkeley; and brother Admekom, a junior in high school.

And there was no way we could know that in 1998, in my first year as a professional runner, the children would combine resources to buy a home in San Diego, allowing my parents to get out of low-income housing and a bad neighborhood. We will never be able to repay what our father and mother have done for us. My parents are our heroes. They have been the ultimate role models in their love and devotion to each other. They have inspired us with their selflessness and hard work. They never settled for the convenient. They overcame incredible obstacles to reunite our family. And they never stopped trusting that God would provide for our family if we continued to acknowledge Him.

Our family celebrates our arrival in America every October 21. It's a big day for us, almost like New Year's. It's an anniversary that has grown in significance over the years as we have accomplished more here. We send e-mail messages to those who can't attend the celebration. It's a time to take stock of our situation, to realize how far we've come, and to encourage each other. We don't take the opportunities here for granted.

We children did not have that grand perspective on October 21, 1987, when we left Rome and arrived in San Diego. I was a 12-year-old kid excited to see relatives whom I had heard about but had never met. Fitsum had heard that America was heaven—everyone had a villa. Not just a home, but a villa. Imagine.

Once we landed, we learned the airlines had lost the luggage that contained my parents' traditional Eritrean clothing. So we didn't have much more than the clothes on our back. None of us except my father knew any English. Still, we had traditions from our native country. We had each other.

We were together in the Land of Opportunity, which did become like heaven for us.

RUNNER'S TIP
If you're eager to improve, be careful about making too many changes or changes that are too severe. Be careful about adding mileage and increasing speed. Too much too soon usually leads to injury. Think gradual, not drastic. Think long term, not immediate.

OVERCOMER'S TIP
Learn everything you can in the classroom. Then go out into the world and learn even more.

3.0 / COMING TO AMERICA

FOR MORE THAN TWENTY YEARS, the centerpiece of my parents' living room has been a golden plastic trophy shaped like Aladdin's lamp. That little award, no bigger than my fist, tells all you need to know about what education means to our family.

We arrived in San Diego in late October 1987, after the school term had started. We spoke no English and were enrolled in English as a Second Language classes, though there were no teachers who spoke our native Tigrinya.

So we were starting from behind, to say the least. My older brothers, Fitsum and Aklilu, were in ninth and seventh grades. I was in sixth grade. My sister Bahghi was in fifth grade, my brother Merhawi was in second grade, and my brother Bemnet was in kindergarten. We were surprised to be placed in different grades. We figured we'd all be starting out together, as beginning students, because that's the way it would have been done in Eritrea. We thought by being together we could help each other. Once we discovered we would be apart, it remained our goal to all do our best, but there were obstacles—academic, linguistic, cultural, and economic.

Fitsum had at best a fifth-grade education based on his Eritrean and Italian experience. He was starting four grades above that, in the middle of the semester, and, worst of all, he knew no English. Yet at the end of the school year, Fitsum earned a top ninth grade student award at Roosevelt Junior High. My parents have proudly displayed his little trophy in our living room ever since. We have earned hundreds of other trophies and medals, but none are displayed as prominently.

It was our most rewarding moment. All of Fitsum's hard work had paid off. He provided us with a great example and hope—if we worked hard, the rest would follow. My parents had preached that bit of wisdom for years in Eritrea and Italy. Now we saw it in action in the United States. Maybe we *could* take advantage of the Land of Opportunity.

My parents made sure we worked hard academically. Though money was an issue, we were not allowed to get jobs during the school year because my parents wanted us to focus our time and energy on academics. As soon as we arrived home from classes, we would change our clothes. We didn't want them getting dirty midweek; we had no washing machine and so on weekends would go to the Laundromat, where, of course, we studied during the washing and drying cycles.

As soon as we had changed, we started our homework, which continued before and after dinner. There was always homework, even if there were no assignments due or we had completed them at school. There was always something that could be done. Not that we'd always want to do it. When the younger kids, who often had less homework, had finished and would begin wrestling or begging to go outside to play, Dad would stop them. "Read, read. You can never do too much."

My father instituted 4:30 a.m. English lessons that lasted for several months until our knowledge of the language began to surpass his. He had us work through a big English-Tigrinya dictionary, trying to improve our vocabulary and spelling. Spelling was difficult for me. After taking a test early in the week, we'd get the corrected paper back and then be tested again on the same words on Friday. It was all so foreign to me that I didn't catch on that we were being tested on the same words twice each week until later in the year. Then I studied my mistakes more carefully. I relied on memorization, studying the sequence of the letters, and writing each word a number of times. I didn't miss many words on Fridays after that.

No TV was allowed during the school week, but we had weekend privileges. We'd watch cartoons, which were an important way to improve our command of the language. My father would watch with us, saying, "Repeat, repeat" after certain phrases.

My father followed the same standard in his jobs—taxi driver, janitor, restaurant worker—that he held us to academically. He stressed that whatever we did, we were to do it the right way, pay attention to details, and make the extra effort. He did not want us to settle for less than the best in our efforts and goals.

We saw that he lived what he preached. I often wonder what he would have become if he had had the advantages of education he provided to us. The man has a photographic memory. He remembers incredible details about people and events. He's writing, in Tigrinya, the story of his journey from Eritrea to Sudan, Italy, and the United States. I think he would have been a great interpreter because of how he was able to pick up Amharic, Arabic, Italian, and English in addition to Tigrinya and some dialects. Merhawi thinks he would have been a great lawyer or judge, considering how he successfully navigated the immigration bureaucracies and always advocated for fairness.

////////////////

After a week with our sister Ruth, her uncle Rede Tewelde, and his wife and daughter, we were able to move into our first apartment on Arizona Street. There were three bedrooms and one bathroom for two parents and seven kids. You learn some lessons, other than showering quickly, in an environment like that. You have to plan ahead—when you can use the bathroom, for example. You have to pay attention to details—placing things where they won't get lost or taken by the younger kids. All that was perfect preparation for eventually running the marathon, which requires careful planning and attention to detail.

When the family first arrived, we were on welfare until my dad could find a consistent job. We used food stamps to purchase our groceries. I was in line once buying some food and milk and a package of batteries. I had no money and assumed I could use the food stamps to pay for everything. When it came time to pay, I pulled out some food stamps. The cashier informed me that they were good only for food, not anything else like batteries. I pretended to rifle through my pockets like I had forgotten my money. How embarrassing it was to feel everyone's eyes on me as I put the item back! Tough, but I had been through worse.

We learned some good lessons about delayed gratification from the family approach to material goods. My father's message was "If it's necessary—shirts, pants, pen, paper—ask for it. If we have the money, we'll get it. But don't have the audacity to ask for things when you should know better. 'Dad, can we have a car?' I don't have the means to get you whatever you desire." We weren't familiar with common English expressions at the time, but later we learned to appreciate sayings like "Is it a need or a want?" and "Live below your means."

While we may not have had much materially, we were rich in relationships. Eritreans value spending time together and helping one another out. That was true in San Diego, just as it had been in our village in Eritrea. Furthermore, in the coming years, my uncles Beraki, Asfaha, and Abrahaley all ended up in San Diego with their wives and kids. Amoy Letemichael would travel back and forth between Italy and the United States to visit family, including her daughter Teberh, another sister to us, and Teberh's husband, Alazar. It was as if we had brought a little piece of our village in Eritrea with us to San Diego. We would get together at each other's homes for different celebrations.

///////////////////////

One of the best parts of moving to 2838 Arizona Street was that we were about a half mile from Morley Field, the northern part of Balboa Park, the largest urban park in the country.

We would dribble a soccer ball—we now had a real one instead of a makeshift one—down the street and play pickup games on the grassy fields at Morley. My father was finally able to play soccer in a park with his kids. My brothers and I loved soccer. My nickname in Italy was Pelé, and I quickly regained the name in the United States. I was a striker who loved to score. I still remember a bicycle kick I scored on during an indoor game—my body ached for a couple of days after a hard landing on the wooden gym floor.

I played on indoor and outdoor soccer teams all through junior high school. At first I wasn't even aware that running was considered a sport. Often on Saturdays at Morley Field, lots of people would gather to run a race. My brothers and I had never heard of cross country or track and field. What were these people running for? we wondered. There was no ball. What were they chasing? It made no sense to us.

One weekend there were more festivities and excitement than usual. Turns out it was the Kinney Cross Country Championships, a meet for the top high-school runners in the country, which is now called the Foot Locker Cross Country Championships. It seemed like a big deal, but how was I to know about sports in the United States? I didn't even know about the Olympics.

My dad did stress fitness, mainly because he thought it would help us study and get better grades. He wanted a balance between school and exercise. There was a fitness course at Morley Field. We'd run from station to station, where signs directed us to do designated exercises—push-ups, sit-ups, squats, jumping jacks.

The first time I ran seriously was for a grade. In seventh grade phys ed class at Roosevelt Junior High, we did some running around the school grounds for a few weeks. Then the PE teacher, Dick Lord, told us we were going to be timed running the mile and receive a grade. "If you run hard, you're going to get an A or a B. If you goof around, don't pay attention, or don't try hard, you're going to get a D or an F."

I was always striving for an A, so I ran hard. I can still diagram the course on paper. It passed through the school grounds, on dirt and on concrete, up and down ramps, all right next to the San Diego Zoo. I just ran hard because I wanted that A; I had no idea of strategy or pace. My time was 5:20. We ran the distance on a few more occasions that year, and my times lowered to 5:17, 5:13, and 5:10. Lord phoned San Diego High School cross country and track coach Eduardo Ramos: "We've got an Olympian here." A PE class had turned my life around, though I didn't know it at the time.

My favorite sport was still soccer. I began playing against adults in weekend games that were part of Eritrean get-togethers in the San Diego area. But the older players didn't like it when some pint-size kid was outmaneuvering them and making them look foolish. Plus, I was pretty small then and the play was aggressive and competitive, so my father worried that one of them would break my leg or otherwise injure me. So I started sitting out the games against adults. Instead, I'd run laps around the field while they were playing.

Soon I became more interested in running. Fitsum and Aklilu were running at San Diego High and having success. It looked like fun. We have pictures of me lurking in the background during team huddles before races, trying to listen to Coach Eduardo Ramos giving the team strategy.

///////////////////

Academics remained the family's top priority. If there were extra credit assignments, all of us did them. Grades were divided into two parts. Students got the usual letter grade, A through F, for academic performance; there was also a citizenship-conduct-effort component where you could receive an E (excellent), G (good), S (satisfactory), U (unsatisfactory), or N (Needs Improvement). We were expected to get an A, E for every class. A note that I still have from Mrs. Pais, my seventh grade advanced math teacher, sums up what most teachers thought of me and my siblings:

6/22/89

Dear Mebrahtom: I'm sorry I was unable to use your extra homework certificates to improve your grade. The "A, E" you earned is difficult to improve!

It's been such a pleasure to have you as a student this year. Students like you, and there aren't many I've come across, are what makes teaching worthwhile. If all my students would work just half as hard as you do, what a beautiful world this would be!!!

I thank you for your hard work, questioning mind, and the family that has raised such a fine young man.

The faculty loved us. Not all the students did. During eighth grade, I had a run-in with a member of a Mexican gang. The kid deliberately took my seat in class. I moved to another desk, but I knew this kid wanted to create trouble because he followed me to whichever desk I moved to, more than just once. He came over, told me to move, and said, "What are you gonna do about it?" We started shoving one another, and I knocked him down. We were sent to the principal's office, and both of us were suspended. My father came to school and asked me what had happened and why. When I explained, he told the principal, "My son should not be suspended." I was still suspended, but my dad wasn't mad at me.

At times we were objects of ridicule. We had Afro haircuts when we first arrived. Kids would yell, "What's the deal with your hair? You think it's the seventies?"

We didn't have many clothes, and those we had were European style, much more tight fitting than the baggy U.S. style of the time. We took some grief for that, though looking back, I'm not so sure why. I have a photo from Europe that shows me, at about 11, wearing a plaid shirt, jeans, and a sweater tied around my neck, Italian style. All the clothes were secondhand, but my wife thinks it looks like a Polo ad. "You don't look poor," she says.

We had strategies to maximize our school outfits by sharing clothes and mixing and matching shirts and pants. It worked great when we were in different schools; it was a little harder to pull off when we were in the same building.

In addition to our clothes, classmates would joke about our shoes. We shopped at Payless and bought knockoffs of top brands, such as Pro Wings. We'd buy shoes at least a half size too big to accommodate growing feet.

///////////////

In ninth grade I joined my brothers Fitsum, a senior, and Aklilu, a sophomore, on the San Diego High School cross country team. I was not at SDHS, which is grades 10 through 12, but I was allowed to compete for the school. I attended Memorial Academy, a feeder school to the International

Baccalaureate program at SDHS, a curriculum designed to expose students to college-level courses. I caught a school bus at 5:30 a.m. almost a mile from my house, meaning I had to get up at 4:45, which was practically sleeping in now that our 4:30 study sessions had ended. After school, I'd take a bus from Memorial to SDHS, about a three-mile trip, and then, after practice, go home with my brothers. We'd study until about 11 p.m. before going to bed, and then get up and do it all over again.

Coach Ramos told the *San Diego Union*, "I think sports is like the fun time for them. When they're in school, they go to the classroom, they go the library, they go to the lab. When they're at home, they have more homework."[2]

And sports was a good way for me to assimilate myself into a new culture. Participating in sports gave me an identity other than the kid with a hard name to pronounce. I was the fastest kid at school. People were giving me high fives. Sometimes the compliments came with more teasing: "You were running from the lions and tigers. That's what made you fast." After the first year, we had learned English well enough to communicate more. Prior to that, we were so quiet that other students thought we must be stupid.

In high school, I attended Anytown USA, a retreat for high school students designed to teach cooperation among different people. I wrote an essay about my experiences, mentioning that one day I might want to write a book to help other ESL students:

Social life is also difficult because of language barriers. Even if you are the most interesting person in the world, you need to be able to carry on a good conversation to relate to people. Also people start to judge you this way and that way, even before you have said a word. I also found it very difficult to communicate to the best of my ability when people made fun of me and my accent. This was especially very true in the early stages of learning English. To deal with problems like these I think it's best to not be shy. What worked for me was I got involved in sports. Once the students saw me run and play soccer, they started to be friendly and introduced me to their friends. Also, I found it best to be open-minded about other people instead of making assumptions about them or their character. . . .

In my book I want to communicate to ESL students that I understand being a student of that nature is difficult. Nonetheless they need to take advantage of the opportunities available to excel in life. I would ask them to accept the challenge, and I would hope my book would inspire them to succeed.

I needed help to succeed and was beginning to find it. One family that was instrumental in my development was the Van Camps, whose daughters Noelle and Gretchen ran on the SDHS cross country team. Steve Van Camp, a cardiologist who had run track in college, and his wife, Gail, were very involved with the cross country and track teams. They'd drive us to meets and host the annual team banquet. In addition to the sports connection, we shared a deep belief in Christ. Not only did they help me navigate through high school, they have remained friends and trusted advisers throughout my life.

They've always cared about my education and future; there was no vested interest in it for them. Throughout the years we haven't always agreed on everything, but I know they always have my best interest in mind. They have been friends in the truest sense of the word.

When we traveled to out-of-town meets, I would usually sit in the front seat next to Steve, who would make me read the newspaper aloud. He used to say, "Everything I've learned, I've learned through athletics. You can learn so many things from following sports in the newspaper. And it's a good way to learn English."

When I got to a word I didn't know, I'd circle it. Once I got the definition of a word, Steve or Gail would have me use the word in a sentence. As I started winning more races and attracting more attention, the Van Camps worked with me on my media skills. They'd conduct mock interviews with me. I couldn't answer just yes or no, I had to expand on my responses. I can still hear Gail telling me, "Slow down and e-n-u-n-c-i-a-t-e so that everyone can understand you, because you have an accent." They taught me how to deflect some questions so I could bring teammates into the discussion. They told me to have fun and that if I was easygoing with the media, they would be easygoing with me. Most of my press skills and public speaking skills come from them. I'm thankful for all the hours we put in and for their willingness to work with me.

Sometime during high school, the Van Camps approached my father, explaining that I had a future in college running but needed to shore up my academic skills to ensure a scholarship. They offered to help in any way they could. Because they asked permission to help me rather than saying, "Meb needs to come here and do this," my dad did not feel threatened. He knew they could provide some help that he couldn't.

So on many Saturdays and Sundays, they picked me up and brought me to their house in Mission Hills, which I still consider a dream home in a dream neighborhood. After studying, I would usually help Steve do some yard work and then stay for their traditional Sunday spaghetti dinners. Steve was always offering me sports and inspirational books to read: *The Jim Ryun Story;* John Wooden's *They Call Me Coach Wooden*; and *Pre: The Story of America's Greatest Running Legend, Steve Prefontaine*. To Steve, I became like the son he never had.

The Van Camps let me use their computer to write my papers. Gail would help me with writing. "Go back and try again" was her usual comment. I got used to seeing lots of red marks on papers. As I got older, Gail quizzed me in English in preparation for the verbal part of the SAT. She felt the SAT verbal test was unfair for someone still learning English, so we worked hard on vocabulary. During my senior year, she was my personal teacher for English class. She'd come to SDHS two or three times a week for special sessions with me. Instead of reading the advanced books some of the other seniors were assigned, I studied something more appropriate for me and would write a paper about it. She didn't make it easy on me, but I didn't expect her to. At the end of each marking period, Gail and the teacher talked and agreed on my grade.

Things were easier when it came to running. About midway through my freshman season, I became the number one man on the team, ahead of both Fitsum, who was injured in the first part of the season, and Aklilu. The three of us placed 6–9–12 in the California Interscholastic Federation–San Diego Section

Championships. Our team took first place and qualified for the state meet.

My freshman year I also won the league title and finished 25th at the state cross country meet, the first freshman across the line. But that's not what I remember most about the year. There were a couple of other important moments.

During a trip home from a track meet, I had a conversation with an older teammate, Jose Perez, who was also a good soccer player. He told me I could be a good soccer player but a much better runner. That helped me decide to drop soccer and concentrate on running. While watching Fitsum and Aklilu play soccer, I had seen them encounter difficulties with playing time or teammates. I didn't want to deal with similar frustrations outside my control.

The individual nature of running appealed to me. You start at the same place with your fellow runners. You all finish at the same place. How you do is largely up to you. If you win, you congratulate your team and yourself. If you lose, you evaluate how to improve. You can't make excuses like "He didn't pass me the ball" or "The coach didn't put me in." It's on you. That's the beauty of the sport.

The highlight of my freshman year came at the year-end banquet. The teachers took up a collection to buy me a new pair of ASICS shoes and a letterman's jacket—the name Keflezighi took up the entire back of the jacket.

Getting the jacket was huge—I still have it. At the banquet, I remember Mike Anderson, the father of teammate Jason Anderson, telling me, "You'll make a beautiful marathoner one day." At that point, I didn't even know how far the marathon was.

COACH EDUARDO RAMOS: The faculty loved the young man. They loved all the Keflezighi boys. Out of the goodness of their hearts, the teachers bought the shoes. We've got a lot of needy kids at our school. Once in a while, when those kids superachieve, we get them a letterman's jacket on their birthday or Christmas or some other occasion. Sometimes parents say, "This cost a lot. You didn't need to do this." I say, "No, your son or daughter will appreciate this forever."

As I continued to run, I met others who helped me. Ron Tabb, who was one of the top American marathoners in the early 1980s, was a local junior college coach whom I got to know as a sophomore. I did some eight- and ten-mile runs with him. When I had some Achilles tendon problems, he did massage and other therapy to help me heal. He also told me I was destined to be a marathoner. He had run the marathon in under 2:10. I picked up a lot of useful information from him during our runs and conversations, including learning that the marathon was 26.2 miles. *Way too long for me,* I thought. He predicted I would make the Olympic team in 2000 in the 10,000 meters and get a medal in 2004 and 2008 in the marathon.

Coach Tabb used to train me and other local high school runners, including future Arkansas runner David Levy from Mission Bay High School, during the off-season. He was demanding as a coach. If we were supposed to run 400 meters in 66 seconds but ran it in 63 or faster, he'd make us do it again. (That happened once—we learned our lesson.) It was

RON TABB: I had the opportunity to train and coach Meb during his junior and senior years, evaluating his strengths and weaknesses. Though he was the number-one ranked high school runner in the country, I felt he didn't have the necessary speed to be a world-class 1,500-meter runner. I told him, "You and I have a lot of similarities, and I think you'd be more suited to be a 5,000 and 10,000 meter runner in college and eventually move up to the marathon." On some of those eight to ten-mile runs, we'd get down to a 5:10 or 5:20 pace and he was able to maintain it. That's the reason I told people he eventually would become a marathon runner.

okay to go slower than goal pace. It was not okay to go faster. He wanted to teach us a sense of pace, discipline, and patience. He wanted us running faster at the end of workouts than at the beginning, mimicking what we'd do in a race.

///////////////////

By the fall of my senior year, I had made enough of a name for myself that colleges were recruiting me. I chose UCLA, which offered me a full scholarship (more about that in the next chapter). Signing with UCLA in November was a relief. So was successfully taking the SAT.

In order to be eligible for a scholarship, I had to score a minimum of 700 combined on the SAT verbal and math sections. I had an excellent GPA, about 3.80, but the SAT was a problem. The verbal part killed me on my first try, even with all the help from Gail Van Camp. It was almost like my strategy for that section had to be eenie, meenie, miny, mo—guess at one of the four choices. I wasn't using strategies like "there's the Latin root" to determine the meaning of a word. And to me the analogies section then was like post-run ice baths are now—I hated them, but I had to do them.

In October, I took the SAT again instead of going to an invitational cross country meet where I was defending champion. I didn't want to do it, but I knew it was necessary. I wound up scoring above the qualifying score, so I was eligible for a scholarship.

With the necessary score and signed letter of intent, I could concentrate on my big goals for senior year—state and national titles.

At the state cross country meet, I had finished 25th as a freshman, 17th as a sophomore, and 3rd as a junior. I was hoping for a title as a senior as well as a berth in the Foot Locker Cross Country Championships. I had been watching that meet since seventh grade; now I wanted to run in it after barely missing qualifying as a junior.

I had a teammate, Jose Melgar, who helped push me in workouts and races. We often went 1–2 in dual meets and invitationals. And there were plenty of other good area runners like future UCLA teammate and roommate Devin Elizondo and David Levy of Mission Bay, Mark Hauser of St. Augustine, and Nazario Romero of San Pasqual. I could not get complacent, or I would be beaten—San Diego had turned into a hotbed of distance running. So the summer before my senior year, although I was motivated to run, I stuck to conservative mileage totals of about 50 miles per week. But they were quality miles.

I was unbeaten in cross country by the time of the California Interscholastic Federation–San Diego Section Championships

---

COACH EDUARDO RAMOS: Meb was our hardest worker and would always rally the team. After he finished a race, he would go back down the course a quarter of a mile or so. Then he would cheer on his teammates. Kids notice things like that. That's one of the reasons he was such a popular young man.

---

at Morley Field, the qualifier for the state meet. I set a course record for the 3.1 miles, finishing in 15:04.5, nearly 20 seconds better than the old mark and 55 seconds faster than I had run it as a freshman. Jose finished second (15:43.6).

"This was just a hard workout today," I told the press. "I can run a lot better with competition. My goal was to go undefeated this season, and so far I've accomplished that. Last year, I'd just go, 'Zoom.' I didn't have any strategy. I have more maturity."[3]

My third consecutive section title made me the favorite for the state meet in Fresno. I took the lead from the start to win the Division I race on the 3.1-mile course in 15:02, the fourth-fastest time in course history. My post-race comments indicated my thoughts: "Two down, one to go. Now that I've finally won a state championship, I want a national title."[4]

A week later I was back in Fresno for the West regional qualifier for the Foot Locker meet. The top eight make it to nationals; I had finished 10th the year before, a near miss that added to my training motivation.

After I went out with leader Matt Davis of Spokane, Washington, I finished third (15:01) behind Davis (14:53) and Matt Farley of Sacramento (14:57). I was pleased with my consistency, running one second faster on the course than I had the week before. I had not made it an all-out effort though. I was saving that for the next weekend at Morley Field.

"I didn't want to do anything stupid and not make nationals," I told the *San Diego Union-Tribune*. "Now I feel I have a big advantage. Morley Field is my home. I run there every day. I'll be able to run the nationals like I did the state meet—to win."[5]

///////////////////////

For high school runners, the Foot Locker meet is practically the Olympics. It was a true national meet in my era, though the establishment of national team championships has hurt the field in recent years. When I was competing, the field consisted of 32 runners, eight each from the four regions of the country. The organizers treat the runners well, bringing in world-class runners as speakers and to interact with the participants and make it a special weekend.

Coach Ramos, Steve Van Camp, and I studied the competitors from the other regionals. I figured five of us would be contending for the title. All of the other four were guys I would become more familiar with during college competition—Matt Davis; Adam Goucher of Colorado Springs; Bob Keino, a son of the great Kenyan runner Kip Keino and an exchange student in Ridgewood, New Jersey; and Brad Hauser of Kingwood, Texas. Some experts were calling it the deepest field in meet history. There was a lot of speculation about me joining Marc Davis, a SDHS runner who had won in 1986, as the second local winner of the race.

About midweek as the excitement was building, some of my family members came down with colds. The Van Camps came to the rescue again. I stayed in their guest quarters, a small apartment above their garage, so I could get some rest and avoid getting sick before the race. After a couple of days at the Van Camps', I moved in to the host hotel for all of the Foot Locker qualifiers, the Hotel del Coronado, one of the most recognizable hotels in the world.

I went out with the leaders. Goucher, running the race for the third time after finishing 13th as a sophomore and 15th as a junior, held back a little on the 5,000-meter course, which was configured differently than the one we ran on for local meets. By mile 2, which we hit in 9:29, four of us were in the lead pack—Davis, Keino, Goucher, and I.

Goucher started pushing the pace. Davis and Keino, both of whom were nursing injuries, fell back. Once Goucher made a big move on an uphill section, I couldn't close the gap. He finished the 3.1 miles in 14:41.7, the fourth-fastest time in course history, and I took second in 14:53.0. The rest of the top five were Davis (15:08.9), junior Brad Hauser (15:09.3), and Keino (15:09.6).

COACH EDUARDO RAMOS: Meb was always very analytical. He didn't just plunge into something. He'd study things and analyze them before making a decision. I thought he was sometimes too conservative in race tactics. I'd tell him, "Just go for it." I thought if he had made an early move at the Foot Locker Championships on the first loop he might have been able to get away because Adam Goucher was in the back of the lead pack at first. The second time around, Goucher made the move. As Meb got older, he started taking more chances.

As much as I wanted to win, I couldn't complain too much about second place. Goucher had more experience—he was running the race for the third time. He had a great day. I was consoled that our West team achieved our goal of winning the team title against the North, South, and East. I was happy for Mark Hauser, who took 11th place and surprised a lot of people.

After the race, my father pulled me into a bear hug and lifted me off the ground. "I'm proud of my son; I'm proud of my son," he said. He knew I had given 100 percent effort. He felt second place in the nation was a big step for our family. A lot of friends and family cheered me on at the Foot Locker Championships, including teachers and students from Memorial and San Diego High School as well as many members of the Eritrean community in San Diego.

My running goals now changed to track, where I had big expectations. In past years, I had been close to titles at the state meet but had never won. I wanted that to change. I thought I had a chance at national titles too. I had plenty of competition in my backyard. As in cross country, San Diego–area athletes would be making noise nationally in the middle distances.

During my senior track season Mark Hauser and I had a great rivalry that helped us both. It started in late March when he used his superior kick and made a big move with 300 meters left to beat me in the 1,600 meters in a local invitational, 4:11.1 to 4:12.0. At that point, we had clocked the two best times nationally. I was slightly less than fresh, having won a 3,200 in 9:08.70 two days before.

Two weeks later I didn't let it come down to the last lap.

I took it out hard with a 59-second lap and made a strong move with 600 left to win in 4:08.32 at the Arcadia (California) Invitational, one of the most prestigious prep meets in the country. Hauser was second (4:09.46), as we once again ran personal bests and the first and second times in the country. Later that evening I finished second (8:59.99) in the 3,200 to Nathan Nutter (8:54.23) of Tempe, Arizona, but was happy I broke 9 minutes for the first time.

In May there was a bigger breakthrough in the 3,200 at the Eastern League meet. Officials were nice enough to accommodate me by moving the 3,200 to the first day of the two-day meet so I could run it before contesting the 800 and 1,600. I went 4:28 for the first half of the race and 4:23 for the second half, with a 62-second closing lap for a time of 8:51.8, which broke the school and league records of Marc Davis, who went on to compete as a steeplechaser in the 1996 Olympics. It was the year's best time nationally. I also won league titles in the 800 (1:55.14) and 1,600 (4:10.63).

The next big race was a May 28 rubber match between Hauser and myself in the state qualifying meet, which was being called the Dream Mile. This time I made a move on the third lap, again wanting to avoid a kicker's duel, and won in 4:06.15. Mark took second (4:13.94).

After the meet, I took my date, Mira Mesa High School's Kiesha Porter, who had won the 110 high hurdles and 300 hurdles at the meet, to my senior prom. Neither of us minded being a little late; we were ecstatic about our wins. I was named king of the prom, one of three Keflezighis so honored. My dad rented a Chevrolet Caprice for me. High school doesn't get much better than a day and night like that.

KIESHA PORTER: Everybody knew how hard Meb worked. I think the biggest reason he was so popular was that he was so humble. The entire family was humble. Many people admired the family and wanted to help them. It was amazing the way Meb would finish a race and then turn around to run back on the cross country course or track to cheer on his teammates—you just don't see that type of thoughtful attitude in high school kids.

The following weekend at the state meet was pretty special too. First, I won the mile. Hauser came by me briefly with 300 meters left, but I figured he had to be tired after catching up to me. I stayed right behind him for a while but then moved just before the final straightaway when I felt Sacramento Jesuit High School junior Michael Stember closing on us. I won in 4:07.67, finishing with a 58.9 final lap. Stember, who became a 2000 Olympian, was second in 4:08.52 and Hauser third (4:08.97).

I tried to eliminate suspense in the 3,200 by making a move with 800 left and finishing in 8:58.11 to win by five seconds over Antonio Arce from Palmdale. The double had been done just twice before in state history. After the 1,600, I took a victory lap, in front of an announced crowd of 9,318, not once but twice, which may have been the first 800-meter victory lap in track history. Maybe I knew I'd be too tired after the 3,200 to take a victory lap. That was a good day's work. The two wins provided 20 points, which tied SDHS for second place in the team scoring.

As happy as I was with my first two state titles, I had to keep focus. I still had two more meets. The following weekend I ran 4:07.75 to win the Golden West Invitational in Sacramento over runner-up and hometown favorite Stember (4:11.26). There was one more weekend left in my high school career, at the National Scholastic Track and Field Championships in Raleigh, North Carolina.

Entering the meet, I wasn't sure whether I would try to double in the 3,000 meters and mile or focus just on the mile. On Saturday night, about 45 minutes before the 3,000, I decided to enter the event. I figured since I'd won both the 1,600 and the 3,200 on the same day at sectionals, I could double at nationals. I went right to the lead, took control, and won in 8:25.07. I had a big test the next day against Seneca Lassiter from Williamsburg, Virginia, who would go on to win NCAA and U.S. titles in the 1,500 meters.

I didn't want it to be a kicker's race; I also knew this would be a chance to become the fourth U.S. high school runner to break 4 minutes and the first since 1967. I pushed the pace early, hitting the halfway mark in 2:00.9, and won comfortably in 4:05.58, a personal best and the fastest prep time in seven years. Lassiter, a junior, was second in 4:07.13.

I was the fastest high school miler in the country.

///////////////////////

When it came time for the senior ritual of signing yearbooks, a lot of friends and teachers alluded in their messages to future glory for me at the Olympics. That was far from my mind. As I prepared for college, academics were still the priority.

I didn't realize it at the end of my senior year, but my identity as a miler was coming to a close. Though I would have loved to break 4 minutes in high school, it wasn't my top priority. Winning state and national titles was. Ron Tabb thought I could have achieved the milestone if I had peaked for it, but I was running invitationals pretty much every weekend—plus school meets on Tuesdays and Thursdays. The bottom line: I was racing too much to be able to focus on one major sub-4 effort.

I haven't run the mile competitively since 1998. It bothers me more now than it did in high school that I've yet to run a sub-4 mile. Part of me still remains a miler.

I have run around the world both in the number of miles logged and the many locations where I've competed. Yet Morley Field remains a special place for me. It's part of my past—it's where I saw running as a sport for the first time; it's where I learned my first competitive lessons; it's where I logged a lot of miles.

And it's still a part of my present running. I go back there regularly to run the same loops I did while at SDHS. Usually I set my goals for the coming year while running at Morley Field. I evaluate the past year and plan for the next. Inevitably I think of all that has happened with my running career and am amazed that I'm still running. That's also a time when I naturally thank God for the ability to run and that He has brought me this far.

Sometimes I'll run past our first apartment on Arizona Street. I have the urge to knock on the door and ask the current tenants if I can look around. I'm curious about how it looks now. I also think about how far the family has come since we lived there. I've never knocked.

I just keep running.

RUNNER'S TIP

If you're serious about running, keep a journal, recording not only your workouts but other details of how you felt during practice. It's a great way to chart your progress. Reading through workouts before a big race can provide a psychological boost.

OVERCOMER'S TIP

Opportunities have a shelf life. Grab them before they lose their punch.

4.0 / UCLA DAYS: STUDENT FIRST, ATHLETE SECOND

AS UCLA COACH BOB LARSEN drove to San Diego in the fall of 1993 for a visit to my home, he kept practicing the pronunciation of my name with assistant coach Eric Peterson. As I would soon learn, Coach Larsen is meticulous with details. He also always has plans. His intention was to offer me a partial scholarship for middle- and long-distance running.

Keep in mind that this meeting came eight months before I ended my high school career with two state and two national titles, which increased my profile as a recruit. Coach Larsen had seen me in a couple of races as a junior, neither of which I had won. He thought I had potential, however, and eventually could help the Bruins.

Then he met my family, which had grown to 9 children by then, and learned more about our story. He had grown up on a farm in Minnesota without electricity and running water, which gave him an appreciation for our work ethic and determination. He changed his mind and offered me a full scholarship.

BOB LARSEN: Kiddingly, I've said I gave the scholarship to the family rather than Meb. Meb was impressive, but the family—wow. They were tough, high-achieving, determined people. Definitely that went a long way in my decision.

That was a leap of faith by Coach Larsen. Full scholarships are rare at the collegiate level because a men's team is allotted 12.6 scholarships per year, not nearly enough to fill out a roster and down from 30 or more grants in the 1970s. Coaches usually dole out partial scholarships in an attempt to attract as many strong team members as possible. At UCLA full rides traditionally were reserved for sprinters or throwers whom the coaching staff felt could provide immediate help by scoring in the NCAA Championships as freshmen. The team already had sprinter Ato Boldon and shot putter/discus thrower John Godina, both world-class performers who would go on to win medals at both the world championships and the Olympics.

I was flattered. But I also felt pressured. I had to make a decision within a week and a half. If Coach believed in me so much, why did the offer come with a time limit? I didn't quite comprehend the scholarship game. Coach was in a tough position too. If he reserved a scholarship for me and I eventually decided to go elsewhere, he might lose a top sprinter or thrower interested in the school. Art Venegas, a top throws coach who was a UCLA assistant and eventually Coach Larsen's successor, told me when I met him, "If you don't take this, I have a thrower who will." I was learning that as you progress up the ladder of competition, the pressure increases for both athletes and coaches.

The home visit by Coach Larsen and Coach Peterson made quite an impression on me and my family. I remember them driving up in Coach Larsen's Mercedes. During the meeting, Coach Peterson did most of the talking. They showed a video about UCLA's academic and athletic tradition. I remember watching clips of Coach John Wooden, Kareem Abdul-Jabbar, Bill Walton, Rafer Johnson, and Jackie Robinson. It was probably one of the most efficient visits in UCLA recruiting history. My younger sister Bahghi and brother Merhawi were so inspired that they wound up going to UCLA too.

The coaches didn't have to sell me too hard. Before their visit, I had pretty much decided that if a University of California school accepted me, UCLA would be my first choice. I had also applied to UC–San Diego and Cal–Berkeley, but I never even heard from Berkeley. I contacted Arizona, but they were more interested in Bob Keino, whom I had competed against in national competition. At Ron Tabb's urging, I also had written to University of Oregon coach Bill Dellinger but never heard back from the coach or anyone else on the staff. No letter, no phone call. (During my senior year, Tabb and I were at an Oregon meet. Dellinger was kind enough to say to us, "Ron, I should have listened to you for once when you recommended Meb. This guy has kicked my guys' butts for four years.")

Harvard was actually the first school to contact me. When the phone call came after my junior year, my father answered. He couldn't have been happier. When the track coach invited me to visit the school, it was like a dream come true for him. He said, "You're going to Harvard."

"Wait a minute. I'm not going to Harvard," I replied.

My father couldn't believe what I was saying. "How can you say no to Harvard? It's the best school there is."

"There's too much academic pressure. It might not be a great fit."

I talked about it with my parents and the Van Camps. I also briefly considered Princeton, which appealed to me more athletically than Harvard. We decided that if I were to attend an Ivy League college, I'd need a year at a prep school in the East. All that additional schooling and relocating seemed too much once UCLA showed interest.

A few days after Coach Larsen met with me and my family, Gail Van Camp drove me to UCLA for an unofficial visit in the middle of the week. Weekend visits were out of the question because we were in the most important part of cross country season with meets on Saturdays. I had to get my father's permission to miss school for the trip. On the drive there, Gail and I talked through my questions and concerns and I wrote them down on a clipboard. On campus we met with the coaches and support staff to discuss issues regarding classes, tutoring, nutrition, and more. All our concerns were addressed.

I liked the campus and team, plus I knew the school had a great academic and athletic reputation. I hit it off with junior miler Dan Niednagel, who is still a friend. (In fact, Dan became a CPA and has done my taxes.) I was sold. In November, before the state cross country meet, I signed a national letter of intent to attend UCLA.

I also felt good about Coach Larsen, who was from the San Diego area. He seemed low-key, yet he had accomplished a lot in his coaching career, including winning two NCAA track and field titles (in 1987 and 1988) and three (later to grow to four) NCAA Coach of the Year awards. San Diegans who knew him told me, "If you go to UCLA, he's going to put his arms around you and take care of you. He's a great guy. " They were right.

//////////////////////

After graduating from San Diego High, I went to UCLA early to take a psychology course and an English course in the summer. That turned out to be a good idea. It got me acclimated to campus life and academics earlier than most freshmen. I ran on my own.

Still, the transition to full-time freshman was difficult for me. The campus had nearly 30,000 students. I was away from my family for the first time, though I could have gotten home within a couple hours' driving time—not that I had a car to do so. But the team and other athletes became my new family.

Josh Johnson, a javelin thrower who is the son of 1960 Olympic decathlon champ/UCLA grad Rafer Johnson, became a mentor. We're the same age, but he was a year ahead of me and more like a big brother. The Lebow family—Jan, Ron, and their young son, Michael—were like surrogate Van Camps, helping me in all kinds of ways. I first connected with them when Jan, the community relations director of UCLA's International Student Center, helped me with some paperwork. There also was a valuable connection to the Eritrean community through my friendship with Mussia Teklemariam and his family. Mussia often came to UCLA to study with me, even though he attended CSU–Los Angeles. I'd go to his house when I needed a fix for *injera*, *himbasha*, and other

Eritrean food and conversation. Devin Elizondo, my cross country rival from Mission Bay High School, eventually became a roommate and good friend, and he still shows up at my competitions to root for me. Kiesha Porter also went to UCLA, so I had a good core group of friends there. Kiesha and I were members of the UCLA branch of Athletes in Action, a Christian sports ministry.

The demands of school and running were a big step up for me. Either one by itself was a challenge; juggling both simultaneously was a struggle at times. I'd get support from my family; Gail Van Camp seemed to always send an encouraging note or a gift just when I needed it.

Make no mistake: as much as I wanted to succeed as a runner, academics were my priority. The guy in charge of student athlete tutorials at UCLA was Tamrat Beyene, an Ethiopian American. Maybe we had some East African solidarity working. He knew I was earnest and could see how hard I was working. He told me, "Anything you need when it comes to tutoring, let me know and I'll make it happen."

I wasn't looking for handouts or for anyone to do my work as some athletes were. I could always hear my father's voice, "Education is something they can't take away from you." I knew no one is able to play a sport forever. Not everyone makes it to the professional level either. During orientation for student athletes, our counselors would encourage us to focus on our studies, telling us that only about 10 percent of us would make the pros. As a runner, I knew the key to success is preparation. It's the same for a student. You have to keep up with the reading, review the material repeatedly, and understand the core points.

I was fortunate that Coach Larsen was just like Coach Ramos at San Diego High School. Both wanted their athletes to challenge themselves academically. Though I heard about easy "athlete's courses" that could help students maintain eligibility, staying eligible wasn't my goal. I wanted to take legitimate courses, progress toward a degree, and challenge myself.

Because our parents had sacrificed so much for my siblings and me, I wanted to make them proud. They could tell how hard I was working. Sometimes my mother would say that I should stop running, that it was taking too much out of me. I told her, "It's paying for my education. It's not so bad. I just have to stay disciplined. God has His plans."

The first thing I did every quarter was check my classes' syllabi against our track or cross country schedule. If there was a conflict with a class or paper or test, I went to the professor immediately. Most of them said, "I appreciate your coming now instead of the week before this is due. I'd be more than happy to help you out." A few professors advised me to find another class.

Throughout my five years at UCLA, I always had an 8 a.m. class. I didn't know there were options to sleep in and still keep up with my busy schedule as a student-athlete—and I wouldn't have wanted them. I did not want to miss class. I'd estimate other than classes I was forced to miss because of travel and competition, I had a total of three cuts in my UCLA career. That's three misses in five years, a great attendance record. I just couldn't live with the guilt of deliberately missing a class.

Two of the misses came because I didn't have my own computer or printer, so I had to wait for something to open up in the computer lab. I must confess to one transgression, however. In my junior year, I cut an afternoon class, Communications 10, to attend a step dance performance at the Bruin Walk, a major campus location. Kiesha Porter took notes for me and our classmate Jaleel White, the actor who played Steve Urkel in the 1990s sitcom *Family Matters*, so we could go to the performance. In my defense, I wasn't totally irresponsible. I arranged to get the notes from the lecture. I think we might even have caught the last 10 to 15 minutes of the class.

My buddies were shocked. "What, Meb missed a class?" The joke with the team and my friends was that if they were looking for me to go for a run or grab a bite to eat, the first place to check was the study lounge of the dorm.

Another typical college distraction—alcohol—was never a problem for me. I didn't touch it, except as part of a toast to be sociable. If I had a vice, it was dancing. I love Eritrean dancing and would go to parties hosted by the Los Angeles Eritrean community every couple of months. I would dance until 3 a.m. I always thought of it as just a little extra aerobic workout. On most nights, though, I'd be in bed by midnight and up by 7 a.m. I couldn't even sleep in on Sundays because my dad would call at 7 a.m. on weekends to check in. When I introduced morning runs to my routine, I had to be awake by 6 a.m. That was still practically sleeping in, compared to my middle school and high school schedule.

I was a big fan of the late John Wooden, the former UCLA basketball coach, and his adages. He used to say the 22 hours after a workout are just as important as the practice itself. You had to take care of yourself by paying attention to what you ate and getting enough sleep. I tried to live right.

My grades meant as much to me as my times. Once I got a C-minus in a calculus class. I was very good at this subject, but went flat on a test just as I might go flat in a race. It was a multiple-choice test; I started running out of time, panicked, and bombed the exam, costing me the grade. I knew I could do better in the class.

I went to Coach Larsen right away. "I knew the material but didn't pass the exam."

"It's okay. Don't worry about it," he said.

"No. I have to get a better grade. I want to take this course again in the summer."

Coach Larsen explained that my scholarship was good only for the regular school year and that I would have to pay for a summer class.

I told him, "If you don't pay for summer school, you might not see me here next fall." He found a way for me to take that summer school course. Now I understand that it wasn't just the class but also the dorms and other stuff that had to be paid for. I think that's the biggest disagreement Coach Larsen and I ever had. Normally I was uncomfortable confronting him, but grades were such a priority to me that I felt this was a do-or-die situation. My sense of urgency was greater than my usual deference. By the way, I got an A in the class the second time.

///////////////

By the time I was a junior, I had to choose a major. I was thinking of engineering. Figures and math were a universal language—like track times—that came easier to me than humanities courses and the nuances of language. However, my oldest brother, Fitsum, who was a talented runner but had elected to be a full-time college student, was an electrical engineering major at UC–San Diego. He advised me against it: "Saturdays are busy for engineering majors. You're supposed to go to the lab and do experiments. It's not going to work with your racing schedule." I was interested in medicine and thought about pre-med, but that's even more demanding than engineering.

I decided on communication studies, which at UCLA is a tough major. When I went to the academic counselor within the athletic department with my plans, I was told, "You can't do this. This is a major for 'elite people.'" My first reaction was anger. Why couldn't I take this? Was it because I was an athlete, an African American, an immigrant, or all three?

I told her, "I know what I can do. This is an opportunity to study something I'm interested in, and I want to pursue it."

To be admitted to the program, I needed a good grade point average, something like a 3.3 or 3.5, and I had to write a letter explaining my interest in the subject. I think there were 450 applicants my year, of whom 100 candidates were accepted, just two of us African American.

It was a difficult major for me, in part because I hadn't lived through relatively recent American events. Also, I hadn't experienced radio or TV until I was 10. If we had to write a paper on Watergate, for instance, my classmates would know much more about it than I did. I'd have to go to the library and dig into the microfilm for background information. If we had five weeks to complete a paper, I started working on it right away. I couldn't do things at the last moment like some classmates. I was proud to finish as a communications studies major. I also took a fifth year at UCLA to get a specialization in business.

///////////////////

When I arrived at UCLA, I had no great ambitions for running. I wasn't fixated on winning a certain number of NCAA titles, becoming a professional, competing in the Olympics, or earning a medal. All that would come later. At first I just wondered how good I could be and wanted to be able to contribute to the team.

Coach Larsen was great with training. His low-key manner is the reason he's still my coach. He's not a my-way-or-the-highway type of coach. Once I got to campus, he asked me about my high school training. I told him about the low mileage and the type of workouts we did. He said, "It's working, so we're not going to change it."

That was so respectful of him. He asked, first of all. He could have taken the approach, "You're in my program now, and this is how we do things here." I don't know if I would have agreed. Who knows what would have happened then? He said, "Let's keep it going and increase the mileage by 10 percent." A wise and sane philosophy.

I had a decent freshman year. In the fall, I finished 15th at the NCAA Cross Country Championships. That was a big deal to me. Coach Larsen had told me that if I finished in the top 15, not only would I be an All-American, I'd be called up to the podium to receive an award.

The way I got 15th place provided an extra thrill. I had gone out hard with the leaders and fell back quickly in the last half mile. With about 300 meters to go, I was 16th and working hard on an uphill stretch. With about 150 meters left, I heard someone yelling at the runner ahead of me, "Come on, Louie." It was Louie Quintana of Villanova. I couldn't believe it. When I was a freshman at San Diego High School, Louie was a senior at Arroyo Grande and won the state cross country meet where I finished 25th. I saw him win some big races, including the 1990 Foot Locker Cross Country Championship title at Morley Field. He was a hero of mine. I really admired him and wanted to be like him. Now I had to beat him to get on the podium. It was funny—he didn't look nearly as tall or as big as I remembered from four years before. In fact, I wondered if that was really him just ahead of me. I sprinted with all I had left and passed him just before the finish. Coach Larsen said I had a huge smile when I went up to the stage.

This contest was also a sign that I was leaving behind, however grudgingly, my identity as a miler. The NCAA Cross Country Championships are conducted at 10,000 meters. My performance indicated I was probably better suited to longer distances, though I kept thinking of myself as a miler who might be able to extend myself to 5,000 meters. Coach Larsen entered me in my first 10,000 on the track at the Penn Relays in April of my freshman year. I wasn't looking forward to it. When we had a discussion about it, I called the 10K "an old man's race." I struggled at the Penn Relays and told myself I'd never run another 10K on the track.

As a freshman in track, I was third in the 5,000 at the Pac-10 meet and fifth in the 5,000 at the NCAA Championships. The NCAA meet had a stacked field; Martin Keino of Arizona, Bob's older brother, was the winner. It turned out to be a sit-and-kick deal, and I really had to pick up my pace

BOB LARSEN: We sat down and I showed Meb splits that he'd need to run 29 minutes. I'd had walk-ons who had done it. Guys were making waves at the NCAA meet running 29. I thought it would be easy for him to do that. I thought he was a good 5K guy who could occasionally drop down to the mile. We could move him around. He was never a high-mileage guy, especially compared to some of the 10K runners. I wasn't going to push it. He had a future in the sport. I didn't want it to be a burden for him to move up to the 10K. I thought he could be very good there.

at the end. The good news was that I completed the last 800 in 1:57, just a second slower than my best in an 800 race. The bad news was that Keino and some others ran 1:53 for the last two laps. Still, I was pleased. I beat my old nemesis from cross country, Adam Goucher, now at Colorado, for the first time. Coach Larsen and I both felt that scoring five points in the title meet justified his decision to extend a full scholarship to me. The only disappointment was that we finished second in the team race, scoring 55 points to 61.5 for Arkansas.

I was in no danger of getting a big head the first year despite some successes. At UCLA you have to earn privileges. I remember asking Coach Larsen before the NCAA Cross Country Championships if I could get one of the big team traveling bags. He said team members needed to be at least all-conference to get one, and I had not officially made the All-Pac-10 team yet. So no bag. I remember thinking, *Wait a minute—I've qualified for nationals and I can't get a bag?* It

made me mad, but it made me appreciate Coach's principles.
Like I said, Coach Larsen was very meticulous on details. I had
a travel bag by track season.

//////////////////////

Sophomore year I learned two valuable lessons the hard way.
The first came through a personal crisis that occurred after
cross country season in late fall or early winter. Suddenly,
UCLA didn't appeal as much to me. I was seeing the dis-
advantages instead of the advantages. I had become more aware
of other colleges and programs and envied some of their assets.
Stanford was emerging as a power, and if I transferred there,
I would have lots of other top distance runners to train with.
Plus that university had a growing program for post-collegiate
distance runners, the Nike Farm Team. UCLA had nothing
similar for distance runners, only for sprinters and throwers.
In addition, Stanford's Palo Alto campus and the surrounding area are beautiful. *You fool! How could you not have even
considered Stanford?* I thought.

In addition, the guys at Arkansas, a school that had won
more than three dozen NCAA titles in cross country plus
indoor and outdoor track, pushed me to transfer whenever
we saw one another at meets. My friend, rival, and occasional
training partner from high school, David Levy, was there,
making the team a more attractive option. They pointed out
the great places to run in Fayetteville and all the teammates
I'd have to train with. "You won't have to warm up alone, cool
down alone, or travel by yourself to all the big cross country
meets." They said I'd be more than welcome on the team,
which planned to continue its dominance.

Meanwhile I was chafing at what I considered the liabilities for distance runners at UCLA. We needed a car to get to the best trails, and I had no wheels. I was forced to run on city streets, dodge traffic, and wait for streetlights to change on busy boulevards like Wilshire, Santa Monica, and San Vicente. At times trees or hedges would extend over the sidewalk, forcing me and the other runners onto the street. We'd tell Coach Larsen, "Tell the city to trim the bushes on Wilshire." Then there was the infamous LA smog—I was on my way to contracting exercise-induced asthma.

I approached assistant coach Eric Peterson about my frustration. At the time, I felt more comfortable talking to him, an assistant in his mid-twenties, than Coach Larsen. It had nothing to do with the coach; it was an issue of my cultural background. The Eritrean way and the Keflezighi family way is to respect elders and teachers. I couldn't talk back to Coach Larsen or challenge him—I just didn't do things like that.

I still remember where we talked, right on Bruin Walk, a campus landmark. We were standing near the statue of the Bruin bear, the school's mascot. I told Eric I was considering transferring. "I'm not sure that I'm really happy here," I said. "I've been the number-one guy since I stepped on the track and cross country course. I'm tired of having to lead all the workouts. I'm not sure all my needs are being met."

"I'm glad we're having this talk. Thanks for trusting me," he said. "But who does Haile train with?"

Bam. His point hit home to me. Haile Gebrselassie of Ethiopia was the world record holder in the 5,000 and 10,000, and he was about to become a two-time Olympic champion in the 10,000. Later he would add the world record in the marathon.

He was a hero of mine. Not only was he dominant, he was a role model—a person with many interests who wanted to help others and improve conditions in Ethiopia. Haile trained largely by himself. Whenever he trained with others, he was always the most accomplished runner.

ERIC PETERSON: I remember that conversation well. I remember telling Meb, "If you perform and compete at the level that we believe you will, who will be able to train with you anyway? You're a pioneer in this program, and we want you to set a standard that is superior to all others. Be a leader and make a name for yourself here."

I explained to Meb that he basically had a personal coach in Bob Larsen, who was fully committed to him. He had Bob's undivided attention, which would prove to be of great value to him. I told him I thought he would be crazy to leave UCLA, that he would be throwing away something special.

I am still grateful to Eric for that moment. Things could have gone sour at that point. But what he told me, I tell students in a lot of my talks today: "It's not where you go, but what you do." I tell them not to choose a school based solely on a sport. Instead, they should go to a school where they will be happy even if, for whatever reason, they can't run.

Eric also pointed out some practical matters. If I transferred to an out-of-conference school like Arkansas, I'd be required to sit out a year of competition. If I went to an in-conference rival such as Stanford, I'd have to sit out for two years. Neither option was appealing. He reminded me that a diploma from

UCLA would have future benefits. It was a deep conversation, and it began to cure whatever was ailing me.

The other learning moment came in the spring at the 1996 NCAA Track and Field Championships. I was coming into the meet as the Pac-10 5,000-meter champion. I felt great in the preliminaries. The team needed me to win for UCLA to take the team title, but I didn't mind the pressure. I told Coach Larsen I was going to break the school record (13:35.00).

I spent the time before the final race visualizing it over and over again. I was so excited. I told myself, *You were fifth last year. You should be able to win it this time.* I slept only a couple of hours that night. I kept creating the race in my mind, seeing myself winning. I got so worked up, I was drenched in sweat.

When it came race time, I was as flat as a pancake. I finished ninth (14:13.71) in a race won by Alan Culpepper of Colorado, who would later become an Olympic teammate. It may have been the most disappointing race of my college career.

Later that summer I learned the probable reason I bombed. I went to the Runner's Workshop at Catalina Island as a counselor for high school runners. There I talked with guest speaker Steve Scott, who held the U.S. record for the mile at 3:47.69 from 1982 to 2007. I explained to Steve, now the coach at Cal State–San Marcos, how I bombed after putting so much energy into visualizing.

He put his arm around me and said, "Things happen." He explained that visualization is important, but that it has to be done in practice a couple of weeks before the race. Runners need to relax physically and mentally in the days right before a major competition. The hard work has already been done or, as we say in track, "The hay is in the barn." I had done the opposite. I had run that race so many times in my head during the roughly 24 hours between the semifinal and final that I was exhausted mentally and physically when I went to the starting line. During our talk, Steve Scott gave me some of the best advice I've ever received. Visualizing is a big part of my training now—but I do it all well beforehand and don't stress out on the eve of competition.

///////////////////

By the time my junior year arrived, other beneficial changes were happening. I decided to add morning runs before my usual afternoon sessions. Even though it meant rising by 6 a.m. so I could meet my teammate Dan Brecht for a run and be done and showered for an 8 a.m. class, the runs paid off. This was another lesson in sacrifice. The winter of 1997 was very wet in Southern California, and if it weren't for Dan, I don't think I would have made it to every morning run. They were nothing drastic, since Coach Larsen wouldn't let me increase my mileage too suddenly, sticking to his 10 percent rule. Still, the morning runs got me up and moving for a few miles four or five times a week.

The additional workouts helped me with my weight, which was between 130 and 135 pounds on a 5-foot-5½-inch frame. At that size I was no big man on campus. But I was trying to become a big man on the track—and that meant dropping a few pounds, down to 127 or less.

I received an eye-opening revelation about my diet in an exercise physiology class I was taking. I had to keep a food diary for a week. I could put food away like an offensive line-man or thrower at the all-you-can-eat dining halls on campus. I could chow down with the likes of All-American shot putter/discus thrower John Godina, a 275 pounder. For breakfast, I'd have a bagel, a waffle and/or pancakes plus cereal. For lunch I'd have a good-size sandwich or pizza and maybe some soup. For dinner I'd have pasta or one of those create-your-own pizzas. There was always dessert, of course. I went for ice cream, especially Klondike bars.

The professor had a jarring message for me after analyz-ing my intake: "You're lucky you have good genetics and that you run because otherwise you would be obese." He suggested some diet modifications. Teammate Dan Brecht and I made a deal—we'd pay each other 25 cents for every bad thing we ate—like cookies or ice cream—or drank, like soda.

Another crucial development came at the start of junior year. Mark Hauser, my old high school rival from St. Augustine, arrived at UCLA after transferring from Wisconsin. I no longer had to lead every workout. I had someone who could push me in speed sessions. He was a tremendous help. He even injected levity into workouts. During repeats he'd yell out, "Goucher who?" or "Wilson who?" referring to two of my main rivals, Adam Goucher of Colorado and Ryan Wilson of Arkansas.

UCLA had recruited Mark before his freshman year, but he told me he had gone to Wisconsin in part because he didn't want me to beat him on a day-to-day basis. When he got to campus, I said, "Let's work together. You can help me and I can help you." Our rivalry in high school forced us to improve; there was no reason the same thing couldn't happen again. He pushed me to the limit. When we did 300-meter repetitions, he'd be running them in 38 seconds. I'm not sure I broke 41. I think I helped him with focus and discipline so he could get more out of his considerable talent, which enabled him to run a sub 4–minute mile once in a workout.

Mark was more than an asset on the track. He helped me with papers I had to write for classes, offering suggestions and helping me organize my thoughts. I still stay in touch with him.

In March of 1997, I won my first NCAA title, at 5,000 meters indoors. It was a convincing win that gave me a boost in confidence. At UCLA we did not treat indoors too seriously. We'd do a couple of meets, using the season to prepare for outdoors. Any title was just frosting on the cake.

I went into the outdoor season with confidence, a leaner frame, and more speed than ever. Three months later, I had a major breakthrough. My outlook on track and my future was changed over 50 laps in less than 72 hours as I won the 10,000 and 5,000 meters at the NCAA Outdoor Track and Field Championships in Bloomington, Indiana.

Going into the meet, I was not the favorite in either event. But my goal was to win both. I thought I could run really fast in the 5,000—sub-13:20, maybe even sub-13:13. We had done a 6 x 800–meter benchmark workout that gave me confidence. For the half miles, I went 2:04, 2:02, 2:00, 1:58, and 1:56 for the first five. The last one was all out, and I went 1:53. So I knew I was ready.

The 10,000 came first, on a Thursday evening. I won it going away, finishing in 28:51.18. Brad Hauser of Stanford was second (29:02.58) and Ryan Wilson of Arkansas third (29:06.81).

The 5,000 semifinals were Friday. I felt good and advanced

BOB LARSEN: Meb and I had talked about the fact that you have to be mentally ready but you can overdo it. In those days I would try to get him and anybody else I coached to relax. I knew if I could get them to smile a little bit before a race, they'd be loose and relaxed. I didn't even have to say anything that day. He smiled at me as he was stretching before the race in all that rain. I knew he was going to have a good race and those other guys were in big trouble.

comfortably. I didn't stress out or overvisualize on the eve of the Saturday final as I had done as a sophomore. Coach Larsen told me, "The pressure's off. You've already won the 10K. Stay relaxed." It was raining for much of the final. He told me to not worry about the rain and to keep my face relaxed so that the rest of my body would relax.

The final was a grind. With about three laps to go, I made sure I got away from Goucher and Wilson. They both could kick. I thought, *I've got to go early.* I had learned in high school the value of putting the hurt on guys early. It takes the sting out of their kicks. Goucher went with me and tried so hard to catch me that he blew up and finished third. Wilson passed him late. I finished in 13:44.17 with Wilson at 13:46.18 and Goucher at 13:49.85.

I felt I had progressed to a new level with the double win, becoming the eighth runner to win both the 5,000 and the 10,000 and the first since Brigham Young University's Ed Eyestone in 1985. My thinking began to change: *Maybe I can do this professionally. Maybe I ought to consider the Olympics.* I was finally catching on to what the Olympics were. In 1988,

shortly after we arrived in America, I was oblivious to the Seoul
Games. I was slightly more aware of the Barcelona Games in
1992. I actually paid attention to the '96 Games in Atlanta. I
was very inspired by Bob Kennedy's bold early move to take
the lead in the 5,000. Josh Johnson brought me a T-shirt from
Atlanta with the flags from the participating countries. His
father, Rafer Johnson, actually lit the Olympic Flame in the
1984 Olympic Games in Los Angeles. UCLA had a rich track
and field tradition, and I was catching Olympic fever. I was
beginning to think running could be a job.

I even thought briefly of forgoing senior year and turning pro.
That became a trend about five years later when distance runners
like Alan Webb and Dathan Ritzenhein left school early, but it
was rare when I was a collegian. As I considered that option,
though, I remembered that the reason I had come to school was
for an education. There was a competitive reason to stay for my
senior year too. Even though I felt I had accomplished a lot in
track, I still hadn't won an NCAA cross country title.

Then, all of a sudden, I couldn't run. Shortly after that
spring NCAA meet, I wound up with a stress fracture in my
right foot. Maybe it was the 50 laps in 72 hours—who knows?
Whatever the cause, I was not going to be doing much running over the summer. There would be no great buildup for
my final season of collegiate cross country. We had to change
plans. For Coach Larsen and me, the only target for cross
country was the NCAA Championships. Any other meets I
ran beforehand would be tune-ups. I would have to get in
shape during the regular season.

At Pre-Nationals, a race held on the championship course
in the month before the title meet, Goucher smoked me by

45 seconds or so. I didn't panic. I had trained through it. The week before I put in 85 to 90 miles, so I hadn't tapered by cutting back on my mileage. Again, the only goal was nationals.

I trained through the Pac-10 Championships too. I was defending champion but no match for Washington State's Bernard Lagat that day. With about three miles left we were running together when I got a painful side stitch. I remember thinking, *I can't beat this guy today.* Again, my focus was on the championship meet at Furman University in Greenville, South Carolina. I gained a bit of confidence by winning the district title and beating Lagat in the last meet before nationals.

The field was formidable for the November 24, 1997, NCAA Championships. There was Goucher, whom I had never beaten in cross country and who would win the 1998 title; Lagat, who would represent both Kenya and the United States internationally and win multiple medals in the Olympics and world championships; Arizona's Abdi Abdirahman, who has made three U.S. Olympic teams; and Michigan's Kevin Sullivan, who has made numerous world championship and Olympic finals in the 1,500 for Canada.

I went hard from the start on the 10K course. We went through two miles in something like 9:08. At about four miles, I turned to Bernard and said, "Let's go. Let's go." He replied, "My side is hurting." I knew how he was feeling. *I guess I gotta go now,* I thought.

I took control of the race. I remember hearing Coach Larsen yelling, "Watch out for the roots." He thought the only way I was going to lose was if I tripped on one of the large, exposed tree roots on the course.

It might have been the most memorable win of my college

career. The 5/10 double a few months before had been special too. But cross country always meant a lot to me because of the diverse competition. You had milers plus 5K and 10K guys in there. The fields were always deep.

Looking at a picture of the top finishers in that race now, it's impressive to see how many good runners there were, knowing what they went on to accomplish. I finished in a course record of 28:54 followed by Sullivan (29:01), Lagat (29:05), Goucher (29:10), Wilson (29:13), Nebraska's Cleophas Boor (29:22), Abdirahman (29:26), Stanford's Nathan Nutter (29:34), Arkansas's Sean Kaley (29:39), and Stanford's Brad Hauser (29:42). Farther back in the field were a couple of other guys who would make world and Olympic teams, Stanford's Jonathan Riley in 23rd and Alabama's Tim Broe in 40th. That was a high-quality win against at least eight future Olympians.

What added to my satisfaction that day was that Steve and Gail Van Camp had traveled from San Diego to attend the meet. Fitsum, my oldest brother, was there too. That meant a lot. I don't know if I would have been a runner if Fitsum and Aklilu had not done so first. My brothers showed me the way. The Van Camps assisted me. It was a gratifying moment for all of us to be there.

STEVE VAN CAMP: After the race, I called Meb, "Champ." I told him he looked great. We embraced. "Happy birthday," he said. He's always thinking of other people and remembering things like birthdays. Once Gail hugged him after he crossed the finish line at the New York City Marathon and he told her, "Happy birthday."

I had just won my third NCAA title in six months. The only others to win the 5/10 cross country trifecta in the same calendar year were Washington State's Gerry Lindgren (in 1966 and 1967) and Texas–El Paso's Suleiman Nyambui (1980), who is a native of Tanzania. I had become what Coach Larsen called "the chasee." I was no longer the chaser.

//////////////

The rest of my senior year did not develop the way I wanted or expected despite some good early signs. During outdoor season, I recorded a personal best in the 1,500 of 3:42.29 (equivalent to a 4:00 mile) plus school records in the 5,000 (13:26.85) and 10,000 (28:16.79).

But I did poorly at the NCAA Championships in 1998. For openers, I took fourth in the 10,000. My plan was to make an early move, but I abandoned it because I wasn't feeling great when it was time to go. I decided I would make a move with maybe a lap left instead. That was a tactical mistake. With 600 meters left, three Stanford guys jumped me. Brad Hauser; his twin, Brent; and Nathan Nutter went flying past me like they were riding bicycles. It was a shock to my body and my mind. I was thinking, *I can understand one person from the same university, but three? Wow.* I tried to fight back but had nothing.

I was battling food poisoning in the 5,000 prelims the next day. When you're a college kid and traveling, you don't always eat at the best places. I think the culprit might have been a meatball sandwich. Anyway, I got through qualifying but didn't have much left for the final. I wound up fourth, just like in the 10K, this time behind Goucher, Abdirahman, and Mike Power of Arkansas.

BOB LARSEN: Meb had just come off one of the best calendar years any collegiate distance runner ever had. I'm not sure he could get back to that same emotional level. It's hard to repeat; you become the target. It changed the mind-set. Certainly Meb was still determined. He maybe had lost that little edge he had the previous year. That little difference became a major difference in trying to pull away from good runners. I think he was ready to run fast, but he didn't quite have the sharpness to pull away from those guys. When it came down to the end, they were a little faster.

As I look back on those disappointing finishes, I know I was still intent on winning. I had used poor tactics in the 10,000— I should have gone much earlier as planned—and I was feeling rotten during the 5,000. Nevertheless, the results were extremely deflating for me. And it put a damper on my start as a pro athlete. Had I been able to win one of those races, I think shoe companies would have been more aggressive in bidding for my services. Instead, my performances created questions about my potential.

My last college meet was a disappointment, but my overall career was not. I had gone from a miler to a distance runner with four NCAA titles. I had won in every discipline—cross country and both indoor and outdoor track.

It wasn't easy being a distance runner at UCLA, but it was the right choice for me. I had a great coach turned friend and mentor in Bob Larsen. I had a great academic experience, which would be extended for one year as I got a specialization in business. I made some great friends I still stay in contact with.

And now I was ready to turn professional.

RUNNER'S TIP

Most recreational runners could benefit by spicing up their workouts instead of doing the same old run every day. Once a week do a longer run. On another day, make the run, or at least a portion of it, faster than usual.

OVERCOMER'S TIP

Before making a decision, step outside the situation to get the best perspective.

5.0 / TURNING PRO AND LIVING SMALL

JUST LIKE A LOT OF COLLEGIANS who sign their first professional sports contract, I splurged on new digs and new wheels. Only for me it was a little different. My new housing was a one-bedroom university apartment just off campus that I rented with two other runners, steeplechasers Matt Pitts and Dan Brecht, for the 1998-1999 academic year. My only stipulation on the rooming situation: No top bunk because I didn't want to fall.

I was taking advantage of the fifth-year scholarship option UCLA originally offered in 1994 in order to finish my degree in communication studies and add a business specialization. Even though my collegiate eligibility had expired, Coach Larsen would still train me. The only difference was that I could get paid for running now.

The wheels came when I forked over 50 bucks to Coach Larsen for his 1973 Ford LTD, which he was considering donating to Goodwill. I must have been a sight on the road. I was a little guy driving a big boat that was two years older than

I was. I needed to sit on a pillow to see over the steering wheel. The trunk was so big that if I needed to reach something in the rear, I actually had to climb into the trunk to get it. I got some new hoses and belts for the engine, which had about 60,000 miles on it. James Menon, one of my training partners after college, tuned it up for me, and the car was good to go. Living below my means, as far as I was concerned, was better than living large.

When some friends bought new cars, I was tempted to do the same. But I had seen how Coach Larsen and the Van Camps had acquired wealth by living below their means. There were other reasons for economizing as well. I wasn't making much money, though I had enough so that once I graduated, I didn't have to get a full-time job. Instead I could train full time for the first time. There was no school to worry about. In 1999, after getting my degree, I entered in my training log, "It's time to give running a 100 percent commitment." It was what I wanted to do. I was looking forward to all the extras like regular massages and more ancillary training that I didn't have time for while I was a student. I wanted to up my mileage. I was excited to work as never before and see where it took me.

Though I didn't know how I would fare professionally, I figured this was the time to give running my all. While at UCLA, I'd had a couple of opportunities to meet John Wooden. He defined success as the peace of mind that comes with knowing you have done your best. He didn't talk to his teams, which won a record 10 NCAA titles, about winning. Instead, he emphasized playing to their potential and getting the best out of themselves in practices and games. That made a lot of sense to me.

One highlight during my college years came in 1998, when I was able to visit Coach Wooden at his home. Doug Erickson, who worked for UCLA basketball, and Bill Bennett, a sports information officer at UCLA and a friend of mine, arranged it. I will never forget the coach's advice to "surround yourself with good people and good books." After hearing that, I took special note of the volumes on his bookshelves. I spotted books by or about Mother Teresa, Martin Luther King Jr., and Abraham Lincoln. I remember seeing some lighter works, too, such as *God's Little Instruction Book* and *Chicken Soup for the Christian Soul.* I spent about two hours with him. He was a kind, warm man who was knowledgeable about many subjects, including track since the trainer for many of his championship teams was Ducky Drake, who was also the head track coach at UCLA during that time.

In the summer of 1998, after I had finished my athletic eligibility but before I had completed my schooling at UCLA, I wrote shoe companies seeking sponsorship. Bill Bennett, Steve Van Camp, and Coach Larsen helped me compose a letter that I sent to Alberto Salazar, a hero of mine, at Nike; Reebok, which was then a UCLA sponsor but had just spent much of its elite-athlete budget on Canadian and former University of Michigan runner Kevin Sullivan; and ASICS, a Japanese company that sponsored U.S. athletes.

I introduced myself and said I wanted help in becoming a world-class runner. Here is part of the pitch I used:

Now that I have completed my collegiate eligibility (I will graduate in Spring 1999), I want to focus even more on running and maximize my potential to a higher level.

*I hope [insert name of shoe company] can help me reach
my goal of becoming one of the best distance runners in
the world. I think I would be a great addition to your
company because I have good character with versatile
athletic ability. In the near future, I am confident I will
make a positive contribution to U.S. distance running
in the 5,000m, 10,000m, road races, and marathon.*

I customized the letter to Nike and Salazar, mentioning
that I had followed his career and that he was an inspiration.
John Capriotti, on behalf of Nike, made me a first offer for
$15,000 a year. I acted as my own agent, with advice from
Coach Larsen, and they eventually upped it to $30,000. I seri-
ously considered ASICS and might have signed if they had
offered $15,000 for the entire year, rather than $7,500 for
the remainder of that calendar year. The reason I would have
accepted a lower base from ASICS is that their bonus clauses
were more attainable and their contract did not have reduction clauses as severe as Nike's. Reduction clauses are a reality
in running contracts. If I did not meet certain standards of
time or placement, Nike could greatly reduce my base pay.
I didn't like that; who would? What if injury or illness, not
complacency, caused a bad year? I didn't think it was fair to be
punished financially to such an extent.

Still, I signed with Nike. They were at the time—and still
are—the biggest shoe company in the sport. They're everybody's dream. I figured if I could hit it big, they would have
the ability to market me the way they featured Bob Kennedy,
who had the Nike Zoom Kennedy shoe named after him. Of
course, that was a big *if* for me at the time.

In 1998, I had another issue besides finding a shoe sponsor—my citizenship and the country I would compete for. I was about to obtain U.S. citizenship, which was great. But since I would have dual citizenship with Eritrea, the question was, which country should I run for in international competitions like the Olympics and world championships?

It was a major decision—almost up there with who to marry—that could have major repercussions on my life and career. And it was a difficult choice. I was torn, and so was my family. The timing of the decision added to the difficulty. By then I had spent about half my life in each country. I had allegiances and connections to both. It was the biggest decision I ever had to make as a young man.

Running for Eritrea would give me the opportunity to represent my family's roots and that nation, which had finally won independence after 30 years of war. If I chose Eritrea I was virtually guaranteed selection for their Olympic and world championship teams. In fact, I could probably name my event and compete for the country for a long time. The disadvantage was that Eritrea was new to international sports and its track federation was newly formed and inexperienced. Eritrea did not send any athletes to the 1996 Atlanta Olympics. Running for Eritrea would mean greater difficulty in navigating my new professional career and finding sponsorship.

The situation was reversed with the United States. There are no guarantees of making an Olympic and world championships team here. Officials don't select the U.S. teams; athletes try out for them. If you finish in the top three at the Olympic trials and have the international qualifying time, you earn a spot on the team no matter how unknown you may be. If you're a world record holder or gold medalist and are injured or ill at the wrong time and finish out of the top three, then too bad: you don't make the roster. It can be cruel, but it's probably the only way to run things in a country that has such depth of talent.

The advantage of running for the United States is that, for all the problems with national governing bodies, we still have a well-funded sports structure. The U.S. facilities are great. The marketing and endorsement opportunities are great. The sports medicine is great.

But could I make the U.S. national teams? I was far from dominant at the time. I had some promise. I had won some NCAA track titles but none senior year. I had seen two U.S.-based athletes I knew, sprinter Ato Boldon from UCLA and 400 meter hurdler Felix Sanchez from San Diego and the University of Southern California, be successful competing for their native countries—Trinidad and Tobago for Boldon and the Dominican Republic for Sanchez.

Whatever decision I made, it would be costly to reverse. Once you represent a country internationally, you usually must wait a couple of years before you can represent a new country in a major championship. I didn't feel I could afford to lose any time, so it was crucial to make the right decision the first time.

In 1997 I was approached by Eritrea to represent the country at the world championships. I could have been the first Eritrean to carry a flag at a major international competition. It was a tempting honor, but I turned down the chance. First, I didn't feel I was in great shape—I didn't even run the U.S. meet after the hard collegiate campaign that ended with NCAA titles in the 5,000 and 10,000. Second, I didn't want to get locked into representing Eritrea prematurely.

Picking a country to represent weighed on me. Several nights I didn't sleep much, thinking about it. I prayed for the wisdom to make a wise choice. The family was divided, almost like Democrats and Republicans split along party lines. My father, Fitsum, and Merhawi, were lobbying for Eritrea. Fitsum was an electrical engineer and offered to house me and support me if I couldn't get a shoe contract while running for Eritrea. "We'll find a way and make it happen," he said. My mother said to follow my heart.

MERHAWI KEFLEZIGHI: You have to respect Meb's decision-making process. He thought about the pros and cons deeply. He didn't just go with a piece of his heart. He didn't rush the decision. He looked at the long term and the short term. I was highly disappointed at the time. Ultimately the decision he made has been the best for both countries. Within the family there was a lot of love and respect. Even if he makes a decision that is averse to what I want or Dad wants, he will still have our support.

Finally, I elected to go with the United States. In the end, it was a no-brainer, even though there was no guarantee what kind of career I would have. On my mother's advice, I went with my heart: I had been here a long time, I spoke the language, I had gone to school here, and I wanted to be dedicated to the country. I also figured there were too many athletic and financial opportunities in the United States to ignore. Some people in Eritrea were mad that I didn't run for them and felt I was dishonoring the country by my decision. I meant no dishonor or disrespect to Eritrea, which is a big part of who I am. It was a difficult choice, but I made the best decision possible and am proud of it.

I knew that if I became the best athlete I could be, it would reflect well on both countries. I felt that competing for the United States gave me the best chance and support to get the best out of myself. I look at it this way now: Every time I'm mentioned in a story or on television, Eritrea is also mentioned. So I've helped Eritrea be noticed.

One UCLA professor who frequented school track meets told me, "Meb, you should run for the world. Have a special designation." That would have been fun. Then if I won a medal, three countries could claim me—Eritrea, Italy, and the United States. I am a citizen of the world, but I do represent the American dream.

I became a U.S. citizen on July 2, 1998, at about 10:15 a.m. in San Diego, just missing doing it on the Fourth of July. It was a day I will never forget. The setting was incredible at Cabrillo National Monument, atop a bluff on Point Loma, with the Pacific Ocean on one side and Mission Bay on the other. They should have been playing, "America! America! God shed His grace on thee."

I was among 153 new citizens, seated next to a 91-year-old guy from Mexico who had lived in the United States for 72 years. It doesn't matter if you're 23 or 90; you want to become a U.S. citizen. It has so much meaning.

At one point the presiding judge called the roll of the nearly 30 countries our group represented. He asked if there had been any omissions. I stepped forward and said, "Eritrea."

I'm proud of both countries. Sometimes I wonder if

Americans born here take their situation and advantages for granted. To prepare for my U.S. citizenship, I was given a study sheet with 100 possible questions that I might be tested on. As I prepared for my exam, I also started quizzing teammates. I knew more answers than most of them.

A little more than a year after I got my citizenship and a few months after I graduated from UCLA in 1999, I moved to the U.S. Olympic Training Center (OTC) in Chula Vista, California, about 15 miles from downtown San Diego. I was grateful to be accepted. In fact, I was the first distance runner to live there year-round. I had a place to live for free and access to sports medicine specialists, sports psychologists, physical therapy, and a dining hall, where the food was even better and more plentiful than at UCLA. It made focusing on running easy, though I had to be careful about my diet.

My roommate was Tim Seaman, one of the top U.S. racewalkers. He and the other racewalkers drew maps for me so I could find the best routes to run on the trails. That was great, although there was one problem early on. I was out on a run in unfamiliar territory when I spotted helicopters overhead. I figured the activity had something to do with crackdowns on illegal border crossings. Soon I heard gunshots nearby. I put my hands up in surrender, thinking immigration officials mistook me for a border crosser, and then heard more shots. I hit the dirt, having flashbacks to Eritrea. When nothing else happened, I ran back to the OTC and told people about the incident. They laughed. "Sorry, we forgot to tell you to be careful. It's duck hunting season."

The center was about 35 miles from my parents' home in Mira Mesa, a San Diego suburb, so it was easy to get home once

or twice a week. I'd work five nights a week at the center as a
cashier and customer service representative to pick up a little
money and take a break from running. You can't do anything—
running or sleeping or studying—24-7. This helped provide a
little balance to my life, as did a writing and speaking course I
was taking from Gail Van Camp, who had started a tutoring
business. I was trying to add more than running to my résumé.

Living and training at the center provided the focus I needed to
make the 2000 Olympic team. I entered the trials in Sacramento
with confidence. I had started the year with a string of 100-
mile weeks that ended because of knee tendinitis. Still, I was
able to finish seventh at the U.S. cross country championships
in February and made the U.S. team for the world championships when Adam Goucher dropped out. At the worlds in Faro,
Portugal, I took 26th, the top finisher for the United States.

I was pleased with the finish, considering the injury. I was
overjoyed to see an Eritrean team there and interact with the
team members. For the first time in my life, I was talking to
Eritrean runners. We danced to Eritrean music. I gave them a
lot of advice on training, diet, and drills. I would have loved
to coach them.

After the meet, I took a planned break to visit relatives and
friends in Italy, whom I had promised I'd visit when we left
Italy years before. I saw Amoy Letemichael Tewelde, my sister
Ruth's mother. She showed me around Milan. I met with one
of my former classmates in Monza, Marta Menin, who is like
a sister to me, and a friend from UCLA, Bindi Patel, who was
teaching in Italy. An Italian teacher of mine from childhood,
Maestra Angela Lippe, burst into tears upon seeing me again
and showed me all of the Christmas cards and letters I had

written to her in Italian and sent from the United States. She kept the cards in a drawer next to her bed. Psychologically, I went back to my roots. It was great way to relax before the coming challenge: making the Sydney Olympics team.

There was one more enjoyable experience before competition turned serious. President Bill Clinton visited the Olympic Training Center in June. He was great at interacting with athletes. I had my picture taken with him and later bumped into him unexpectedly. I introduced myself, told him I was from Eritrea, and thanked him for helping broker a peace treaty between Eritrea and Ethiopia, which had been at war again for the past two years. I also asked him to be fair to Eritrea. He said he was working hard on it. For that brief moment, I was sure I had his complete attention. He knows how to connect with people, both in groups and individually, an ability I admire and want to improve in myself.

Before the trials, I planned two 5,000 races, hoping to earn the Olympic A qualifying standard of 13:29. In Eugene, Oregon, I was awful, running 13:48. I was much better in a meet at Stanford, running a personal best of 13:30.26, just missing the standard but giving myself confidence.

My attitude for the mid-July Olympic trials was to remember the hard preparation I had put in, be thankful I was healthy, and leave the rest to the Lord. Early in the meet, I hit a home run in the 10,000. I viewed my major competition as Alan Culpepper and Abdi Abdirahman, rivals from my collegiate days. The plan with Coach Larsen was to remain patient the first 5K and then to make a move with about two miles left. That's what I did, throwing in a 63- or 64-second quarter with eight laps left. They let me go. I couldn't believe it. With a lap to go, I had a lead of about 8 or 10 seconds. I thought I had it won easily with 200 meters left.

As I hit the final straightaway, I could hear the crowd cheers getting louder. At first, I thought the noise was for me; after all, I did have a lot of family members, who had driven up from San Diego that morning, and Bay Area friends there. Then I realized it was for Culpepper, who was rapidly gaining on me. The sound was incredible. As I shot up my right arm in a victorious gesture, I could see Culpepper right behind me. The next moments were like slow motion. I leaned forward, hoping to beat him to the finish. I asked someone if I had won. "Too close to call. A photo finish," I was told.

The next few moments were excruciating until it was announced I had won in 28:03.32 over Culpepper at 28:03.35. Three one-hundredths of a second apart. The race had a closer finish than the 100, where Maurice Greene (10.01) edged Curtis Johnson (10.07). I had trouble sleeping that night—not because I had won but because I was afraid I had somehow lost. The good news was that in addition to being on the Olympic team, I had achieved the Olympic A standard, recorded a personal best, and received a nice bonus from Nike for winning a national title.

I was going to the Sydney Olympics. And I didn't have to chase a qualifying time. Coach Larsen and I decided against entering the 5,000. With a team berth already secure, we played it conservatively, not wanting to risk injury. I had finally reached a level a lot of my friends from high school had assumed I would. I never assumed it would happen, as you can tell from the all-capital-letter entry in my journal: USA NATIONAL CHAMPION. I AM AN OLYMPIAN.

Making the U.S. team had been a big *if* when I was debating what country to represent, but I had done it.

After the decision to skip the 5,000, I focused on relaxing. With some other runners I made my first trip to Yosemite National Park. I went on a seven-hour hike and run there with former UCLA teammates Dan Niednagel and his then-fiancée and now wife, Beth Bartholomew, whose strong Christian beliefs have always had a positive effect on me.

Coach Larsen and I debated about whether I should make a trip to Europe to compete in a race or two in August. Thankfully I decided to go. In Hechtel, Belgium, I ran a personal best of 13:11.77 in the 5,000, moving up to number four on the all-time U.S. list, just ahead of Alberto Salazar. Before running a 10K in Brussels, I was invited to a dinner at the Eritrean embassy. I loved the food, laughs, and discussion we had about the collective culture of Eritreans. While there I met prominent Eritrean poet Reesom Haile. After watching my race in Hechtel, he wrote a poem in Tigrinya about me: "Sydney, get ready for Meb." Dr. Reesom lived in Belgium and I would visit him and his family during my future competitions in Europe until he passed away in 2003.

My momentum continued in Brussels. I didn't get the 27:39 I was hoping for, but I did break 28 minutes for the first time, however barely. Then it was back home to get ready for the Games.

I was feeling a new sense of peace about my career. My mother often told me and my siblings, "You have to think ahead and prepare, but ultimately it's God who will finish the job." Very early in my career, I may have been tempted to think I could succeed on my own. However, before long I realized that while God expected me to use the tools I had to meet my goals, the final results were up to Him. During this time, I wrote in my journal, "My preparation has been great with the Lord taking control of my life. . . . First, my family has been supportive. Second, Coach Larsen has been there during rough times. Third, the Van Camps have been there when I need anything. The Eritrean support has been phenomenal."

Just before we left for Sydney, the Van Camps hosted a party for me that included my family, Coach Larsen, 10K teammate Abdi Abdirahman, and OTC people, plus friends, coaches, and teachers from high school. The lesson I learned from that was to always be myself and keep in touch with special people. I was honored as much by a party organized by the local Eritrean community. They had long been supportive of me, going back to when they got me running shoes when I graduated from high school. I told them, "God is working His power through my running."

Once we got to Sydney, the Australians knocked themselves out with the opening ceremonies. I was more than happy to march; a lot of veteran athletes opted out in order to rest.

In the semifinals, I advanced and broke 28 minutes for a second consecutive time, despite not feeling great. My mom and dad came to Sydney, thanks to a Budweiser program that brought in parents of Olympians who could not finance the trip on their own. My brother Fitsum paid his way to Sydney, and Merhawi's trip was arranged by friends who were working abroad in Australia. Additionally, Ron Lebow kept his promise to come to Sydney if I made the Olympic Games.

Before the final, my father told me, "You're going to win." He thought I was going to beat Haile Gebrselassie of Ethiopia and Paul Tergat of Kenya, who had staged an epic battle at the 1996 Olympics and were favored to do so again.

I appreciated my father's vote of confidence. Then I tried to explain reality to him. "Maybe some other time I can win. But not here. They're running 26:30s for 10,000, and I just broke 28 for the first time." I believe in setting high goals, but I also believe in being realistic. Some people say you can do whatever you want to do, but I don't think that's always right. Some people don't have the genetics to run a six-minute mile, even if they put all of their mind and body into it.

In the two off days between the semi and final, I came down with a virus that was sweeping through the U.S. team and other athletes in the Olympic Village. For the first time, I wore a Breathe Right nasal strip, desperate to alleviate my congestion. I was just trying to hang on during the race, hoping for a top-10 finish.

As I ran, I did get to watch another stirring Haile-Tergat duel, either by looking across the track or watching on the scoreboard screen. They battled down the final straightaway as in 1996. Just when it looked like Tergat had pulled ahead for victory, Haile surged and was able to defend his title. While I was watching this on the scoreboard, a runner from Mexico, David Galvan, passed me. My attitude was, *I don't care. They may not show a replay of this race and it's too good to pass up.* Once first place was decided, I got back to racing, passed Galvan, and finished 12th. I had run a personal best of 27:53.63. I was 35 seconds or about 215 meters, slightly more than half a lap, behind Haile and Tergat.

I felt great about running a fourth-consecutive personal best, especially because I wasn't 100 percent physically. Before I left the stadium that night, I decided the next time I went to the Olympics I wanted a medal. I was targeting 2004 and Athens. To be honest, I had no idea whether my event would be the 10,000 or the marathon, though I probably was leaning toward the 10K at that time. Whatever the event, I was committed to doing what I needed to get a medal. That goal was set before I left the stadium.

I was able to spend another week in Sydney and party—at least my version of doing so. I hung out with my family and went sightseeing. We had great hosts in Sydney in Sam Tesfay and his sidekick Daniel, who was nicknamed Wedi Keshi. Daniel was actually an Australian in his late teens but had spent six months in Eritrea as a youth while his father served in the Peace Corps. In those six months he had fallen in love with the people and culture of Eritrea. He learned to speak Tigrinya and dance Eritrean. If it weren't for his white skin, you would think he was Eritrean. Sam and Daniel and their community arranged for a party to recognize the first-ever Eritrean Olympic team and invited me and my family to all of the festivities. While Sydney's Eritrean population was not large, many Eritreans lived in Melbourne, and hundreds of them drove more than 12 hours to join in the festivities. The Eritrean athletes in the Olympics that year included Yonas Kifle and Nebiat Habtemariam, two of the pioneers in Eritrean running, and Bolota Asmerom.

///////////////

I entered 2001 with several goals. Among those I wrote in my journal were the following:

For athletics: Get the USA record in the 10,000m. (My goal 27:19.99.)

*Location to stay: Mammoth for altitude training
if applicable.*

*Future: Better investor/start. Look into owning
a house or condo.*

*Social: Have a girlfriend; be engaged by end
of 2001–2002.*

Some of those ambitions would be easier to achieve than others. In April 2001, Phil Price, a former University of Arkansas runner training at the USOTC in Chula Vista, and I piled into my new car. After Sydney, I allowed myself to celebrate by buying my dream car, a Toyota 4Runner. So what if it was used with 40,000 miles; it was new to me. (I gave the 1973 Ford LTD to my father, who kept it running until the summer of 2009.) We headed to altitude training in Mammoth Lakes, California, after running the Carlsbad 5,000, a San Diego–area road race I completed in 13:34, making me think a big breakthrough in the 10,000 on the track might be coming.

Another good sign for me and U.S. distance running was the bronze medal we won in the 2001 IAAF World Cross Country Championships. The team consisted of Bob Kennedy, Abdi Abdirahman, Nick Rogers, Greg Jimmerson, Matt Downin, and me. The team medal was an important early step in the resurgence of American distance running.

I also learned a valuable lesson at that meet. As I was running past fans in the stands, an Ethiopian runner shoved me into the railing. Before I could react, Bob Kennedy calmly elbowed the runner, as if to say, *Don't mess with my teammate.*

By doing so, Bob calmed me down and allowed me to focus on my race instead of the runner.

Coach Larsen, now retired from UCLA, and I thought it was time to try altitude training. It was a staple for most of the top distance runners in the world—Haile and Tergat had lived at altitude their whole lives. I had lived at altitude in Eritrea but had never trained at elevation. In the late 1990s I had considered going to Boulder, Colorado, an altitude training haven for endurance athletes, but decided against it because I knew my '73 LTD wouldn't make it.

When we got to Mammoth, a popular ski resort, it was snowing. I had seen snow before but never so much. I told Phil, "You are from Arkansas. You are doing all the driving." Still, Mammoth was gorgeous. I had been to town previously for training camps that the UCLA cross country team held there for a few days before the start of school. I'd always wished we could move the UCLA campus to Mammoth so I'd have great places to run. We were planning to stay three weeks before racing a 10,000 in early May at Stanford. Jokingly, I told Phil, "If I set an American record, I'm buying a place here."

The three of us—Coach, Phil, and I—shared a two-bedroom condo. Phil and I did long runs, faster runs called tempos, slower recovery runs, and track workouts at anywhere from 4,100 feet to 7,000 feet; the trails at 9,000 feet were closed because of snow. It was tough at first. I felt tired; my body was sluggish. The fastest time I could manage for mile repeats was 4:32, compared to the 4:13–4:16 times I had been recording at sea level the year before.

The 10,000 U.S. record I was chasing was 27:20.56, set in 1986 by Mark Nenow. The mark was almost 15 years old.

I wasn't sure I was ready to break it in May the way I was feeling in April at altitude. It wasn't until Coach Larsen took me back down to sea level at UCLA just before the Stanford race that I could see the benefit of the altitude training. We had been at elevation for 21 days, and now we were doing 300-meter repeats in good times—41 to 42 seconds felt pretty easy. Studies show that longer stays of four to six weeks at altitude provide even greater gains.

Right before the race, I had no accurate read on my fitness. In fact, I had severe reservations about becoming part of a field that was a who's who of American runners. Besides Bob Kennedy, Olympians including Alan Culpepper, Abdi Abdirahman, Nick Rogers, and Brad Hauser were there. I feared a poor performance could hurt my end-of-year ranking and cost me bonus money or trigger a reduction of my contract base.

The morning of the race, I got a call from a friend, Mike Long, an elite athlete coordinator for Elite Racing (now Competitor Group), which conducts the Carlsbad 5K and the Rock 'n' Roll Marathon and Half Marathon series. Mike, a special friend who had done many favors for me through the years, told me he had heard that Bob Kennedy, the U.S. record holder at 3,000 and 5,000, was going for the 10,000 mark at Stanford. "If he's going to get it, he's going to have to beat me," I told him.

At least, I was talking tough. The May 4 Cardinal Invitational at Stanford was set up for Kennedy to get the record by his coach and agent, Kim McDonald. There were rabbits, or pacesetters, to help him establish and maintain his desired pace early in the race. A lot of times when you're trying to set a record like Kennedy was, you come away disappointed.

On the other hand, sometimes when you least expect it, something great happens.

All the pressure was on Kennedy, who like me was a Nike runner. Kennedy, along with Todd Williams, was the hope of U.S. distance running in the 1990s, when American distance running was at a low point. Several top Nike executives were in attendance, including the director of track and field, John Capriotti. For a couple of years I had been asking "Cap" what I needed to do to get a base salary of at least six figures a year. "Go get an American record," he'd always say.

When the race started, I followed Kennedy who was following the pacesetters. They had been instructed to run a 27-flat pace. I was just trying to hang on at first, but things started clicking. I hit the halfway point in 13:35.1 and right afterward passed Kennedy, who later dropped out with about 3K left. The Kenyans in the lead kept surging about every 200 meters. I tried to keep a more consistent pace. I pushed the last two laps, going 65 and 62. As I passed Luke Kipkosgei into third place with about 200 to go, he said, "Not so fast, young man." A little later he passed me.

I wound up fourth, but I knew I had the U.S. record. As I crossed the line, my arms were up, my mouth was wide open, and my eyes were about to pop out of my head. *Track & Field News* got that shot and put it on the cover. It was a longtime goal to make the cover of "the bible of the sport." I had finally done it, but I thought I looked like an idiot, like I had just been electrocuted. My time was 27:13.98, which improved Nenow's mark by about 7 seconds and my personal best by about 40 seconds. Afterward I got a nice call from Nenow, then an executive at Nike. He said he was happy for me and that he thought I could break it again. It was a great birthday gift, as I turned 26 the next day.

(Those are the same sentiments I expressed to Chris Solinsky when, on May 1, 2010, he broke my nine-year-old record and became the first American under 27 minutes, with a 26:59.60. I wouldn't be surprised if that record is broken soon. Besides Solinsky, who was making his 10,000 debut, there are another half dozen Americans I feel can break 27, including myself. I found it interesting that, as I did in 2001, Solinsky stole the show. The race was set up for Galen Rupp who ran 27:10.74, just like my record race was staged for Kennedy. It's tough to try to break a record like Rupp and Kennedy were doing. Solinsky wasn't shooting for the record; he was just racing.)

After setting the record, I had high hopes for the season. At the U.S. Championships, I finished second to friend and long-time rival Abdi Abdirahman. Though I was disappointed, the important part was that I was going to Edmonton, Alberta, for the world championships.

I thought I was ready for a good race in Canada but finished 23rd. I felt so rotten that I knew something was wrong with my body. After some medical tests, I learned I had a parasite. Not only did that news ruin my race, it ruined plans for later in the summer. I had hoped to return to Eritrea with family members but had to pass on the trip, which would have been my first one back to Eritrea.

//////////////////

I made another trip—back to Mammoth Lakes—soon after. This time the move involved more athletes and a bigger plan. We had financial backing from USA Track & Field, the

national federation, plus Running USA, a nonprofit organization founded by different constituencies in the running
industry. That group was heavily funded by road races, led by
the New York Road Runners, who put on the New York City
Marathon. Nike kicked in some money even though there
were non-Nike runners, such as Deena Kastor who represents
ASICS, in our group. That was an unusual gesture in the shoe
industry, where logos rule.

The goal was to revitalize U.S. distance running after recent
low points. In 1999, for the first time in the six decades of *Track
& Field News* magazine, the United States had no man ranked
in the world top 10 of the 800, 1,500, 3,000 steeplechase,
5,000, 10,000, or marathon. In 2000, the United States had
qualified just one man and one woman, instead of the maximum three each, for the marathon in the Sydney Games.

Coach Larsen and his friend Joe Vigil, also a longtime successful coach, were taking a small group of promising runners
to train at altitude. Mammoth would become home for me,
Deena Drossin (soon to become Deena Kastor after marrying
physical therapist Andrew Kastor), and others including Nick
Rogers, Jen Rhines, Matt Downin, Amy Rudolph, and Elva
Dryer. We became known as Team Running USA California.
Mammoth seemed like a good place, though no other top runners were training there. The coaches liked the flexibility. We
could run above 9,000 feet for long runs, or we could go as
low as 4,100 feet to Bishop for shorter, quicker track sessions.
If things got really bad with weather, we could head to Los
Angeles or San Diego. A disadvantage was that there was no
commercial airport, so all of us had to drive six to seven hours
from Southern California to reach our destination. Yet there

was talk about an eventual expansion of the private airport to allow commercial flights, so we had hope for more convenient transportation. The airport did not expand and allow commercial flights until 2009.

The idea was that we needed to have an altitude training base like Tergat, Gebrselassie, and all the Moroccans who seemed to be having success. We also wanted group dynamics to create a synergy among the individuals and create a team atmosphere, as we had in our college programs. Having Bob Larsen and Joe Vigil, two of the most accomplished distance running coaches in America, working together with some of the nation's most talented athletes in a physiologically conducive environment for training was an almost perfect situation. Coach Vigil was a great asset to the team and to me as an individual. His wisdom, love, and approach to coaching are very unique and effective. The thinking was that similar groups around the country could improve our distance prospects. My goal was to become the U.S. counterpart of Haile Gebrselassie. I wanted to try to dominate the 5K and 10K here and then work my way up the rankings internationally. While doing that, I wanted to be a good ambassador for the sport.

At about this same time in 2002, I took a big step that had nothing to do with running. For the first time in my life, I was going to either pay rent or buy a residence. Deena and others gave me a lot of grief. I was 27 years old and had never had a place of my own? True. When I was at UCLA, I had stayed in housing paid for by my scholarship. When I moved into the USOTC in Chula Vista, I also had subsidized housing. I was a professional athlete, but I had never even had my own room, much less an apartment or house of my own.

Coach Larsen and I had talked about sacrifice and commitment. So I thought I would commit to buying a home in Mammoth. I also feared it would be the craziest investment I ever made. I made an offer of close to $500,000 for a home, secretly hoping the sellers wouldn't accept it. But they did. I'm usually a saver, but I understood an investment in a home in Mammoth would be good for me athletically and, hopefully, financially.

Coach Larsen is very real estate savvy, and after looking at the house, he approved the purchase. When he said he'd take it if I turned it down, I was relieved. I also consulted with my brothers and the Van Camps. The deal went through. When Deena, who had a place in Mammoth, bought new furniture, she gave me all her old stuff. The only thing I bought was a bed.

There was another big move in store as well. I figured I'd try the marathon. The year 2002 was what people in the sport call an "off year." There were no summer Olympics, which occur every four years, and no world championships, held the year before and the year after the Olympics. It was an ideal time to scale back training or experiment with new events. It was time to see if all of those early predictors like Ron Tabb and Mike Anderson were correct about my destiny with 26.2 miles.

I committed to running the 2002 ING New York City Marathon in November. The choice was logical because the marathon's organizers—the New York Road Runners—had been instrumental in launching Running USA. I had a good relationship with the NYRR through shorter events they hosted and that I had competed in. No organization has done more to support American distance running and its elite

> **BOB LARSEN:** We really didn't change Meb's training for New York. He was still running 90 to 100 miles per week with a couple of longer runs thrown in. I had guys in the past run good marathons, 2:13 or so, off just track training. We did not want to make this an all-out assault on the marathon.

athletes. Additionally, New York and the United States were still rebuilding themselves after the September 11 attacks. I wanted to support the city's efforts. Also, I was hoping I could do what Alberto Salazar did in 1980 when he made his marathon debut in New York and won. Like Alberto and his coach, Oregon's Bill Dellinger, Coach Larsen and I believed that solid 10,000 training could set a runner up for a good marathon.

I wanted to win and planned to hang with the leaders. Coach Larsen gave me strict orders not to get caught up in the crowd hysteria coming off the Queensboro Bridge and heading up First Avenue through a corridor of screaming fans, a trap that catches many inexperienced runners. But I couldn't help myself. I couldn't resist the urge to go with Rodgers Rop of Kenya and other leaders when they started pushing the pace around mile 16. At about mile 19, I started feeling warm and poured some aid-station water that must have been 38 degrees on my head. Big mistake. My head felt like it was freezing, and my system started shutting down. By that time I also had thrown my beanie away, instead of tucking it into my shorts for possible later use—another mistake. And, of course, my impatience and fast miles on First Avenue were taking a toll.

By mile 21 I was fading, and fading fast. I went from vying for the lead of one of the biggest marathons in the world, to thinking I'd be no worse than fourth at mile 20, to finishing ninth. Late in the race, Ireland's Mark Carroll, whom I knew from his days at Providence College, came by and said, "Meb, let's go." I told him, "You keep going. I am so finished." Rop eventually won the race in 2:08:07. He put about four minutes and change on me in the last five miles. Carroll put two minutes on me in two miles. I had just discovered what hitting the wall meant. I called it getting my PhD in the marathon.

I didn't feel any better when I saw my time: 2:12:35. I had missed the cutoff for my reduction clause with the race organizers by 35 seconds. That meant my appearance fee was going to be cut in half. I also had missed the Olympic A qualifying standard of 2:12. Right after the race I was not the merry Meb most people know.

"You've seen my first and last marathon," I told Coach Larsen. "I don't ever want to do this again."

BOB LARSEN: He didn't know it, but when Meb told me he never wanted to run another marathon, I was chuckling inside. I knew that in a short time Meb would remember the feeling of flying with those guys through miles 17, 18, and 19. That would get him back to the marathon. Plus, I heard the same claim from Meb about the 10,000 on the track in 1995.

When David Monti, the elite athlete coordinator for the race, approached me after the race, I said to him, "I don't want to talk about it. See me tomorrow or the next day."

I was in bad shape—frozen, beat up, and discouraged. My mother was at the finish line with other family members. "No more marathons for you," she said.

Two weeks later, Mom and I were in Eritrea. It was my first trip back since we had left in 1986. We stayed for almost two months and saw more than 50 relatives. I particularly cherish memories of our time with my maternal grandfather, who was 86.

My grandfather told time without a clock. For most of his life, he had used a sundial. But by the time of our visit, he had been blind for about 10 years. Now he had to rely on his sense of the sun's position and the sounds of animals, especially roosters. "It's 3 o'clock," he'd say. I'd check my watch, and invariably he'd be within 10 minutes of the actual time. As always, he constantly told stories and posed riddles.

I did some running while I was there. People in the villages would see me and say things like, "Your heart is going to blow up," or, "Did you miss the bus?" They weren't used to seeing people running and didn't understand competitive running, just as I hadn't when we first got to San Diego.

I would tell my grandfather about some of my runs. He'd ask about what routes I took to certain villages and how long it took. I'd reply and he'd say, "That's impressive." For instance, I ran from our old house to the school we had attended. It took about 15 minutes at an easy pace, so I estimate the distance was two and a half miles. When we were kids we didn't run to school—unless we were late.

"Let me see those legs that are making the world notice," he'd say as he grabbed my legs. When I was a boy, he had taken me to a well where he washed my legs and body with water that was considered holy by the villagers.

Later, my mother and I bathed my grandfather and gave him new clothes and shoes. People came by saying he looked like a new groom. My grandfather died in July 2005, just as we were planning another trip to visit him. I feel so sad that my younger siblings did not get a chance to know him.

My mother and I spent a lot of time in our former village Adi Beyani, which still had no running water or electricity. In fact, the trip was a reminder of how tough life is in Eritrea. Getting what you needed wasn't so easy in the villages. Even in cities, stores and supplies are limited. Even if you have money to buy food, the amount you can purchase is rationed. Sometimes families get up at 5:30 a.m. in an attempt to get bread.

It was a reality check and provided an attitude change in me. I realized how easy we have it in the United States and how tough things are in Eritrea. Suddenly the marathon didn't seem so intimidating.

Life in Adi Beyani centers around growing wheat and producing grain. In the United States, "separating the wheat from the chaff" is an expression; in Adi Beyani it's a process done the old-fashioned way—by hand. I helped relatives bring wheat to an *awdi*, a site where oxen were guided over the wheat to break it up. There's a real art to pairing the oxen so the work is done efficiently. The resulting product is tossed into the wind to separate the grain from the small grass.

The grain is then ground into a flour called *meshela*. The taste is delicious but producing it is difficult. My relatives wouldn't let me get anywhere near the process once we reached the *awdi*. They think Americans are fragile, softened by going to stores where there is an unlimited supply and variety of breads. Their work is painful; their skin itches and hurts from handling the wheat. My uncle Tsgehannes Berhe said he has gotten used to the pain, pointing out that the work is necessary for survival. He said the hardship and pain have made him who he is and that we all have a job to do. I told him I have a simple job, really: to train.

Before leaving, I got a hint at what effect my emerging success as a runner was having on Eritrea. Before a major cycling race in Asmara, officials had me jog 5K along the course packed with people who applauded. I realized that even though I was competing for the United States, any successes I might have would also provide hope to Eritreans. This moment brought tears to my eyes.

The trip put my New York City Marathon experience in perspective: I had it easy. I was privileged to be a professional athlete performing in a sport I love. In Eritrea I got a glimpse of true endurance and sacrifice.

I returned to the States so fired up that I wanted to run the Boston Marathon in April 2003. Coach Larsen knew better and calmed me down. I needed some downtime. The year 2002 had been special for me. I had won five national titles—12K cross country, 10K outdoor track, 8K road, 7 mile road (where I won a car for the first time), and 5K road. I became the fourth U.S. runner to rank number one in the 5,000 and 10,000 in the same year, joining Steve Prefontaine (1973), Alberto Salazar (1982), and Bob Kennedy (1999).

I had purchased my first home. I had reconnected with my Eritrean roots. I was becoming a marathoner.

RUNNER'S TIP
You can do more than get a drink at aid stations in hot weather. Pour water on your head; putting your hat back on afterward can prolong the cooling effect. Use a sponge, first wiping around your neck and then the underside of your forearms and inside your elbows.

OVERCOMER'S TIP
Enrich your life with family and friends who will be there for you in good times and bad.

6.0 / ATHENS . . .
ANOTHER JOYOUS MOMENT

IN OCTOBER 2003, I tried the 26.2-mile distance for a second time—in Chicago, known for its flat, fast course. Unlike New York, I didn't crash and burn at the end. It gave me confidence that the marathon wasn't so awful after all.

Against a strong field, I finished seventh in 2:10.03, about 2½ minutes faster than my debut. I even felt good enough afterward to do a brief jog to cool down. Still, if you want to know how the average 80-year-old feels, run a marathon. It makes you appreciate how you feel normally in doing simple things like going up and down stairs.

The main reason I ran Chicago was to attain the Olympic A men's qualifying time of 2:12, which I did. But the achievement became meaningless when the international track federation later relaxed the qualifying standard to 2:15. If I had known that was going to happen, I wouldn't have run Chicago, since I had met that requirement from my NYC performance the previous year. But I'm glad I did the race because I learned more about the distance. It was a positive experience physically, mentally, and financially.

Because Chicago went so well, Coach Larsen and I had options for getting to Athens, which held significance for me because of our family reunion there in 1986. We targeted the marathon, with trials in February, and the 10,000, which would be part of the track & field trials in July.

I recovered well from Chicago, but once I resumed training seriously in November, I started having some tendinitis, first in the left knee and then in the right. I had to back off. Right around Christmastime I came down with the flu. I just couldn't shake it. The congestion and coughing lingered. At one point in January we considered my not entering the marathon trials because my training wouldn't be adequate. Then, suddenly, I started feeling and running better. When I did a 10-mile tempo run of 48:19 at Bonita Park near the Olympic Training Center, I felt encouraged even though it was not a superfast time for me at sea level. Still, I had no 100-mile weeks, and my longest run had been 20 miles.

I was definitely undertrained, but at least I was healthy going to the starting line. Moroccan native Khalid Khannouchi, who twice set the world record in the marathon and had become a U.S. citizen, could not get to the starting line. He was forced to withdraw because of an injury.

I went to Birmingham, Alabama, with a conservative plan for the February 7 race, which would be held on a five-mile loop course downtown. In the Olympic trials, third is as good as first. The primary goal is to make the team. Winning wasn't really part of my plan, considering my less-than-ideal buildup. I was just hoping to go out there and see if I could make the top three. I wanted to play it smart and be patient on a cold, windy day.

Brian Sell, a relative unknown, made the race. He chased down early leader Teddy Mitchell and by mile 8 was leading on his own. By mile 15 his lead was 58 seconds. That's about the time Coach Larsen yelled at me to take off. There was the possibility of an unfortunate scenario because Sell did not have the Olympic A standard of 2:15. The winner was guaranteed a spot on the team. However, under USA Track & Field and IAAF rules, if Sell won without having made the A standard, he would be the only one to make the U.S. team, even if others had made the standard earlier in the trials qualification period. In order to send the maximum three entrants, all needed the A standard.

No one wanted a repeat of 2000 when there was only one U.S. male marathoner in the Sydney Games. (That runner, by the way, was Rod DeHaven, whom I respect as a runner and person. It wasn't his fault he was the sole U.S. entrant. We needed to have greater quality depth then, and we're getting it.)

Alan Culpepper, Dan Browne, and I led the chase pack. Shortly after mile 22, we caught Sell, who later said, "When they blew by, my hair blew forward." So maybe having hair is overrated. By mile 23, Browne began fading, leaving me and Alan to fight for the win. Both of us were hurting. I had side stitches; Alan was fighting cramps—not that we were exchanging this information with one another right then.

The day before the race, I had run strides on the closing portion of the course, which included an incline and two turns. I wanted to be familiar with the final stretch in case the race came down to a sprint finish. It did. Just as I surged ahead slightly with about 300 meters left, Alan made a decisive move, and ran away from me. He finished in 2:11:42, five seconds ahead of me. Browne earned the final spot at 2:12:02. Mission accomplished. I had made my second Olympic team, and we had the maximum three entries for Athens, who happened to be the three fastest qualifiers in the trials field.

There were some big smiles from the three of us. Alan had his first marathon win; I was on the team again, in a new event; and Dan had just made his first Olympic team.

Sell finished 12th in 2:17:20. I thought he had employed some questionable strategy, such as pushing the pace alone into the wind, instead of letting others break the wind for him. But I also respected his bold move. Afterward I bumped into him and told him, "You know what, next time you will make the team. I wish I had been as fit as I was in Chicago because I could have helped you out in front." He ran a courageous race. (He made the Olympic team in 2008.)

It's nice to make the Olympic team in February; it removes a ton of pressure. Even if I didn't make the 10,000 team, I had an Olympic berth. And I was feeling good after the race. Because of the time I had missed, I think my conditioning was climbing as I entered the trials. I was able to keep it going after a short break, winning the Gate River Run 15K in Jacksonville in early March and the U.S. 8K championship in New York City in late March. I remember Terrence Mahon, who was then transitioning from athlete to coach, encouraging me to take my athletic achievements beyond the national level into international competitions.

Then Alan Culpepper, Abdi Abdirahman, and I won the

three-person team competition on Memorial Day at the Bolder Boulder 10K in Colorado. That was fun because we beat the Kenyans and some other good teams. I told Alan, "I don't care if it's you or me, but one of us has to get on the podium in Athens." Alan and I wanted to train together to prepare for the Olympics in Athens. However, it didn't work out for Alan to join me in Mammoth, and Coach Larsen and I didn't feel that Boulder, where Alan trained, was at high enough elevation to maximize the benefits during training.

Entering the track & field trials in Sacramento in July, I had some advantages. First, I was relaxed because I already had an Olympic team berth. Second, I had a chip on my shoulder. I felt ignored by the media, which seemed to be playing up the angle of veteran Bob Kennedy passing the distance-running torch to the young and promising Dathan Ritzenhein. It was hard to find a picture or mention of me in pre-race articles or the official program. I was defending champ in the trials; I was already on the team in the marathon; I was the U.S. record holder in the 10,000. Where was the love?

Speaking of love, my third advantage came from a special source of motivation. I had fallen for a woman I had met a week earlier at an Eritrean soccer tournament in San Jose. I had never had an official date with Yordanos Asgedom, who was born in Eritrea and had immigrated with her family to Tampa as a child, but we were communicating virtually every day via phone, e-mail, or text message. I knew she'd be watching the final on NBC, and I wanted to impress her. I had a lot of energy going into the event.

On the first night of the meet, I ran away with the title, finishing in 27:36.49, a trials record. Old friend and rival Abdi

Abdirahman was second (27:55.00) and Dan Browne third (28:07.47), just like he was in the marathon. Bob Kennedy, who was recovering from an injury, dropped out of the race. Dathan Ritzenhein, also fighting an injury, limped to a last-place finish. But he was rewarded for his perseverance. Since there were no other race finishers with the Olympic qualifying times, Dathan had the chance to make the 2004 Olympic Team if Dan Browne or I decided to run only the marathon in the Olympic Games. I was in such great shape Coach Larsen thought I might have been able to break 27 minutes that night. But I needed help in leading that I didn't get. Nonetheless, I had qualified for a second berth on the Olympic team.

Now the question for me became what to do in Athens—concentrate on either the 10K or the marathon or try both. Alan Culpepper had already decided to focus solely on the marathon—he didn't even compete in the 10,000. Dan Browne elected to try both in Athens.

My priority was a medal, the goal I had set before leaving the stadium after taking 12th in the 10,000 at the 2000 Sydney Olympics. Coach Larsen and I sat down and went over my potential in the 10,000 and the marathon. Since I had already committed to running the 2004 ING New York City Marathon in November, one possibility was to run only the 10,000 in Athens. I felt I was in sub-27 shape and could contend for a medal. That way I also could give New York a 100-percent effort because I wouldn't be wiped out from the Olympic marathon.

Then again, the marathon might be the best choice. The marathon is the most unpredictable of the Olympic track events because anything can happen when you are running for more than two hours. In Athens, we expected the typically hot, hilly, and humid conditions to neutralize the fastest runners in the field.

The most unlikely choice for me was the double. After all, this was not league, state, or national championships; this was the Olympic Games. I had to give respect to the competitors and the marathon. Trying to do both might prevent me from maximizing my chances in either one. I was haunted by the scenario of running the 10,000 and then finishing fourth in the marathon. I didn't want to be second-guessing myself, asking, *How much better could I have done if it was only the marathon?*

As usual, Coach Larsen gave me plenty of independence, though a decision had to be made in less than two weeks. He said to sleep on each possibility for one night, thinking about it. He told me I was the one who was going to be running the race and that he'd support me no matter what decision I made.

In the end, I opted for the marathon only, which was also Coach Larsen's preference. I liked the idea that we'd be running from Marathon, Greece, to the 1896 Olympic Stadium in Athens, roughly following the route of Pheidippides. According to legend, he was the messenger who ran from the Marathon battle scene to Athens in 490 BC, announced victory against the Persians in what became known as the battle that saved Western civilization, and then promptly dropped dead.

I wasn't committed to dying, but I was committed to improving U.S. distance running. I can remember conversations with Steve Van Camp when we'd talk about what an

American runner in the hunt for a medal late in the marathon might mean for U.S. distance hopes. If U.S. television could show an American vying for a medal late into the race, it could inspire the next generation of runners.

The U.S. coaches and support staff worked tirelessly to maximize our prospects in the heat and humidity of Athens. I, along with Deena Kastor and Jen Rhines, who were part of our training group and went 2–3 in the women's marathon trials, showed up for a multiday seminar on Athens. It was held at my former residence, the Olympic Training Center in Chula Vista, California. All Olympic marathon qualifiers were in attendance except for Dan Browne. We were given an elevation profile of the course plus all kinds of weather data and information on the importance of even, conservative pacing in such conditions. Exercise physiologists Dave Martin and Randy Wilber, both experienced in distance running, had lots of good tips for us. Coach Larsen, named one of the men's team assistants for Athens, had scouted the course personally in 2003 after attending the world championships in Paris. He and Coach Vigil had designed new training routes in Mammoth to simulate the profile of the Athens course.

During those runs, I would be paced by a friend on a bike, Mario Arce, whose brother, Antonio, had been a high school rival of mine. Mario was there every step of the way, dispensing energy drinks and encouragement. He kept telling me I was in 2:05 shape. We'd be doing two-mile repeats at Lake Mary at 9,000 feet, and he'd be yelling, "Paul Tergat's not doing this workout. Nobody in the world is doing a workout like this."

Right after the track & field trials, I headed back to Mammoth

BOB LARSEN: Mammoth is wonderful for training because you can have level running at 7,000 to 9,000 feet. A lot of places in the world, it's all hilly. In Mammoth you can also have rolling hills and really difficult hills. Knowing the Athens course as vividly as I did, we set up workouts with tempo runs that would duplicate what you have to do in Athens. We were running five-minute-mile marathon pace at 7,000 feet over hills that perfectly mimicked the Athens course, so Meb became as efficient as possible at running the pace required for a medal.

for a few more weeks of altitude training. Mammoth weather, with its lack of humidity, is never going to be confused with that of Athens. To simulate the Olympics conditions, Coach Larsen had me wear extra layers of sweats and run at the hottest time of the day. We often drove down to Bishop to run in temperatures that hit 100 degrees. Dr. Mike Karch, a friend, orthopedic surgeon, and ultramarathoner in Mammoth, suggested I sit in the sauna, where I built up my time to a half hour.

Then we headed to Crete, the largest of the Greek Islands and an easy flight from Athens, where USA Track & Field held a training camp at a swanky resort. We had been told that two weeks there would give us 95 percent adaptation to the weather and time change. We went three weeks ahead of time. Coach Larsen had already scouted the area and knew about trails we could run.

We were trying to leave no stone unturned in preparation. We even practiced hydration, drinking from bottles during runs to simulate race conditions. We had been instructed in how to cool ourselves at water stations, pouring water on our heads. We knew to wipe our necks and the undersides of our forearms with the sponges we could get at the water stations to cool our bodies via pulse points.

The training on Crete was going great until about 10 days before the race, when the bizarre occurred. I was attacked viciously by a dog while on a training run with Alan Culpepper; Terrence Mahon, the husband/coach of marathoner Jen Rhines; and Matt Lonergan, the husband/coach of Marla Runyan, a member of the women's team in the 5,000. It was a scary moment. The dog—a German shepherd with a big head and big body—was going for my throat and knocked me over. For a moment, I thought I was going to die. It was surreal. I couldn't believe this was happening to me: I was out for a low-key training run, and some mutt was going for my jugular? And I had thought the real dogfight was going to be the race itself. Were my hopes for the Athens Games going to end in hand-to-paw combat in Crete? I was wearing a heart rate monitor, which showed I was at 110 beats a minute about 10 minutes into the run. Then it spiked to 180 or so during the attack, as if I were in the midst of an interval workout. Alan, Terrence, and Matt had to throw stones at the dog to scare him away. When I told Mario Arce about the incident, he felt bad that he wasn't there for me.

I finished the run despite a bruised back and hip, as well as cuts on my arms and legs. I started seeing a team chiropractor, Dr. Peter Grimes, almost every day. We were staying at a resort on the northern coast, but team doctors didn't want me swimming in either the Sea of Crete or the hotel pool for fear that my cuts would become infected. I couldn't even take my usual ice baths. I felt knee pain climbing or descending stairs.

I could have seen a team psychologist. Instead, I did a lot of prayer and self-talk. I figured God had His plan for me. I was sprinkling *tsebel*, a powder my mother had given me, on my knees. It's chalky, like talc, and comes from ancient Christian monasteries in Eritrea. While there is no magic in the substance itself, it serves as a good reminder of God's healing power. I was sore enough that I took the Thursday before the Sunday race off from running without a guilty conscience. This close to the race, all the hard work had been done. I told myself the incident was just a small bump in the road compared to all that my family had been through.

I got an emotional boost from watching two other races once the track portion of the Games started. Deena Kastor, who had been looking fantastic during our training in Mammoth and Crete, ran a very smart race in the women's marathon, steadily picked off people in the second half of the course, and took third. It was the first medal in the event by a U.S. woman since Joan Benoit Samuelson won gold in 1984. I considered Deena's run a good sign. Not only was it a signal that our preparation and research was working; over the years I had noticed that whenever Deena ran a phenomenal race, I seemed to run one too. Deena was the hope and pride of women's U.S. distance running for many years. The medal she won was a huge boost to U.S. distance running. I hoped to give it another one.

Zersenay Tadese provided an even bigger boost to Eritrea and an unexpected thrill to me by taking the bronze in the 10,000—Eritrea's first Olympic medal and its first in running in any major competition. I was so excited for my native country that I had trouble sleeping. I was getting inspired. When I saw his medal before my race, I told him that I was going to fight for a medal on Sunday. His reply was, "With God's will."

On the way to the starting line for the final event of the Games, I called my brother Merhawi back in California and told him that I had been taking anti-inflammatories for the knee pain and not to be surprised if I was forced to drop out. When Merhawi relayed the information to my parents, my father told him, "He will win through the power of God."

Because of security concerns, I had decided it would be best for my parents and the others to stay home for these Games. I did not want to be worrying about the welfare of family members. I did invite Yordanos, the woman I was courting long distance, to attend, but she didn't think that would be proper— understandable, since we had not been on a date yet.

After I talked to Merhawi, I got back into race mode. I wore a hat and sunglasses to shield my face from the sun. I didn't want to squint during the race because a tight face leads to a tight body and inefficient form. The hat would provide the extra benefit of retaining water poured on my head. I cut my warm-up time by more than half, to about seven minutes, all the while wearing a new Nike product called the PreCool vest. Picture a tight-fitting, sleeveless jacket filled with triangular pockets of water that have been frozen. The ice in the vest cools the skin on a runner's chest and back, lowering blood and core body temperature. Our physiologists said even one degree improvement before the start could help. Coach Larsen went through a lot to find a freezer to keep those vests frozen for all of the U.S. marathon competitors.

Vinny Comiskey, a USOC trainer, had pierced holes in my singlet and cut away the bottom portion up to belly level. Ventilation was key. The idea was to keep me as cool as possible.

As Coach Larsen and I were bused to the starting area, we reviewed race strategy. He didn't need to tell me that I had the 39th best time in the field of 101 runners. He did remind me that nobody would be running 2:04s or 2:05s in Athens. We had data from recent Olympics and world championships indicating that a 2:11 to 2:12 should result in a medal, and many people predicted that 2:15 would be the winning time on this particular Athens course. The conditions on Sunday, August 29, 2004, would not be ideal. The weather was hot; the course was difficult. There was a largely uphill stretch from about mile 12 to mile 20 and then a descent into Athens. "This will work for you," Coach Larsen said.

We caught a break with the weather. The temperatures at start time were in the low 80s in contrast to the conditions for the women earlier in the week when it got well into the 90s.

The field included Kenya's Paul Tergat, one of the greatest runners ever, a five-time world cross country champion, a two-time Olympic runner-up in the 10,000, and the world record holder in the marathon at 2:04:55, which he had run the previous fall in Berlin. Yeah, the course was flat and fast for his record run; yeah, the weather was anything but hot and humid. Still, he was 5:08 faster than my best, or more than a mile ahead of me. To be honest, I didn't think I was capable of beating him. I knew the gold medal was a big goal for him after agonizing losses to Haile Gebrselassie of Ethiopia in the 10,000 in the previous two Olympics.

We had bumped into each other earlier at the Games. Paul Tergat thought I was running the 10,000, but I told him I was doing only the marathon: "I'm just going to try to hold on to you."

BOB LARSEN: Before the race, we drove the course, letting Meb look at it closely. As we got to the finish line, I asked him, "How fast can you run this course?" He said 2:12. I said, "Then you're going to get a medal." He's a good uphill runner, a good downhill runner, and is good in the heat. I was totally convinced he was going to get a medal. I thought he could win. Seldom am I that sure of anybody's chances, especially in an event as long as the marathon where so many things can go wrong and when you've got another guy who's clearly superior to everybody and has an overwhelming time.

Another runner Coach Larsen and I thought would be in the hunt was Stefano Baldini of Italy, who had twice won marathon medals at world championships and had consistently high finishes in major city marathons. He knew how to handle the heat—both in terms of weather and competition.

I had never run an evening road race before. It was kind of weird. I ate at 1:00 at the team headquarters at the American College of Greece, in Athens, where I had been staying. (I stayed there rather than in the Olympic Village to avoid getting caught up in another flu outbreak, as I had in Sydney in 2000.) Usually I have *himbasha*, a sweet, substantial Eritrean bread, before a race, but none was available in Athens. Instead, I ate pasta, bread with honey, and a banana, keeping my intake relatively small.

It was a fine art to figure out what to eat and not eat before an evening marathon.

Alan Culpepper and I talked a little about the race. I decided to include the top of my official USA medal-ceremony sweat-suit in the backpack I was taking to the competition. You don't pack something like that unless you're planning on a medal. Alan didn't take his, but we joked that he could wear mine if he finished in the top three. The only problem would be if both of us medaled.

When the starting gun was fired at 6:00, I tucked into the middle of a large pack that started conservatively. Alan and Dan, who was coming off a 12th place in the 10,000, were nearby. I told Alan that because of the crowded conditions in the pack, I was having trouble seeing water stations, established every 5K, far enough in advance. He used his 6-foot-1-inch height to look ahead and over the pack to alert me to upcoming aid stations. Who says running is an individual sport?

I wanted to relax as much as possible in the early going. I hung out mainly in the back or the middle of the lead pack. Tergat and Baldini were up front, as was Morocco's Jaouad Gharib, the winner of the marathon at the 2003 World Championships, and South Africa's Hendrick Ramaala, a two-time silver medalist in the World Half Marathon Championships, who was notorious for his front running tactics. Coach Larsen was roadside before the 10-mile mark and said "Perfect" as I ran by. I smiled and flashed him a thumbs-up. It was hot, especially when we were running on asphalt sections rather than concrete, but I felt fine.

Shortly thereafter Ramaala made a mini move. I ignored it.

If Tergat had made such a move, I, along with the field, would have had to respond. I also noted Ramaala wasn't running tangents on curves. If he had angled on a straight line toward the curves, he would have saved himself a little distance, another detail that I thought indicated he wasn't to be taken too seriously. I drifted back in the lead pack and we soon swallowed Ramaala, who wound up dropping out.

I was running along comfortably behind the leaders of the pack, not knowing that Brazil's Vanderlei de Lima was making a move. He had run 2:08:34 on a fast Rotterdam course and was a two-time Pan American Games champion who was used to lousy weather conditions. He had to be taken seriously. But at this point I was blissfully unaware. By midway, at 13.1 miles, he had a 10-second lead on the pack that came through in 1:07:33.

By mile 17, de Lima's lead was 29 seconds. Again, I was unaware of his presence way out front. I was excited to be with what I assumed was the lead pack. I felt comfortable with the pace and assured of my tactics because of the nearby presence of Baldini, who knew how to run in the heat and had a lot more experience in marathons than I did. (This was my fourth marathon and Baldini's 17th.) It wasn't until the 30K (18.6 mile) station that I heard from some U.S. medical personnel that de Lima had a big lead of 46 seconds. I thought, *We'd better go. With less than eight miles, I don't know if we can make up 45 to 50 seconds.*

Tergat, Baldini, and I started pushing the pace in the eight-man chasing pack and gradually pulled away from the others. Once we cleared the rest of the pack, I remember looking around and doing the math: *I've got to beat one of these guys to become a medalist.* De Lima had the lead, but we had an advantage. He was doing all the work himself. We could work together to reel him in, which we were doing. The gap was down to 28 seconds at 35K (21.7 miles), where I took water and went through the proper sponge routine.

Up ahead, de Lima's form looked to be deteriorating. Then Tergat began falling behind. I turned to Baldini and said, *"Endiamo primo e segundo"* ("Let's get first and second"). His eyes bugged out. He looked absolutely shocked, like he was thinking, *Is this black dude in a USA uniform actually speaking Italian to me?* I probably should have made a move then and there—he would have been too stunned to respond.

Then one of the more bizarre moments in Olympics and marathon history occurred. At about the 22-mile mark a man dressed in a kilt and beret came running out of the crowd along the street. He grabbed de Lima and pushed him toward the sidewalk until another spectator pushed the interloper away and de Lima escaped. The person who attacked de Lima turned out to be an ex-priest, Cornelius "Neil" Horan, 57, an Irishman living in London. He carried a placard on his chest that read: "The Second Coming Is Near Says the Bible. Grand Prix Priest." The year before he had disrupted a Formula I Grand Prix race by running onto the track, cars whizzing around him.

I had no idea what had happened, although I sensed some sort of spectator-runner disturbance had just occurred as we ran by. I've since learned a lot more about the incident and seen replays. It was a horrible moment. At that stage of the race, you're worried about hitting the wall, you're not think-ing about safety issues. I ran in the middle of the road after that to get away from the crowds. The experience has made me think how vulnerable runners can be to disturbed individuals. Ever since, I've felt some fear when wearing the USA singlet in marathons or road races. Although I wear the USA singlet with pride, I'm afraid it may make me an easy target for some nut.

To his credit, de Lima resumed running, though he later said the incident left him shaken. We continued gaining on him. With about 5K (3.1 miles) left, just as I felt sure we were going to catch de Lima, Baldini surged on a downhill stretch as we went underneath an overpass. I let Baldini go, which may have been a mistake. If it were 3K left, I probably would have gone with him. But it was 5K, a good distance still to go. I was thinking, *You can win a medal, don't blow it.* I was worried that Tergat, a guy who has lapped me in 10Ks, might be recovering from his bad patch and gearing up for a big finish. I didn't realize he was struggling as much as he was behind us.

Shortly thereafter Baldini passed de Lima. I did so about a minute later at roughly the 23.7 mile mark, having discarded my glasses in the setting sun. While making a push to catch Baldini, I threw my hat off with a mile left. In the late stages, he looked to have all the energy in the world. I ran a 4:38 mile and still didn't seem to be gaining on him.

During the last two miles I thought of some of the people who had helped me get where I was—in line to get a silver medal in the Olympics, or a gold, if Baldini suddenly faltered. My life in running began to unfold in my mind like a quick-cut movie scene. The mile in seventh grade PE class. My high school and UCLA teammates and classmates. All my coaches—Dick Lord, Eduardo Ramos, Ron Tabb, Bob Larsen, as well as others who offered advice. The Van Camps. Middle school and high school teachers. Phillip Rangel and his family, who took me to church in San Diego after college and told me I would win an Olympic gold because "you are a righteous man." My parents, Russom and Awetash. Our family journey and our Athens reunion in 1986. I may have run the race, but a lot of people got me to the Olympic Games. I felt my victory was for all the people I encountered on my journey.

Once we reached the finish line on the track in the 1896 Olympic Stadium, Baldini took the gold, finishing in 2:10:55. He promptly dropped to the track, his legs spasming. He had never looked distressed on the course. I was second in 2:11:29, reaching down to pat Baldini and shake his hand just after crossing the finish line. I crossed myself, thankful to God for helping me realize my dream. De Lima finished with a flourish, spreading his arms out like airplane wings and veering from side to side, taking third in 2:12:11. Tergat wound up 10th (2:14:45), Culpepper 12th (2:15:26), and Browne, depleted from the 10K and his legs cramping, 65th (2:27:17).

One of the questions I get the most about the race is if I regret not going with Baldini when he made his move at 23.1 miles. "Why didn't you go for the gold? Why didn't you win it?" people ask. Hey, it's not that easy. You have to make an instantaneous decision out there. There's no coach with you. There's no calling a time-out. It's a snap decision with no consultation. I decided at that point to protect the medal. I knew from my New York debut what can happen in the final miles. I don't think I lost the race as much as Baldini won it. He had a great day. Television coverage indicated he ran a 4:28 mile in the late stages.

The other frequent question I get is whether Baldini and I would have caught de Lima without the fan interference. I'm sure we would have, as Baldini has also said. We were already bearing down on him. But I thought de Lima ran a very courageous race by making a big move to break away from the pack and then getting back on track after the incident. He did a lot of leading by himself, and that's tough. I was really happy that he was able to get a medal.

BOB LARSEN: I think the incident involving de Lima may have hurt Meb's chances. If it had not occurred, then I think Meb and Baldini would have needed a little more time to catch de Lima. I think they would have stayed together longer, working with each other to catch him. They might have been together close to the stadium or even on the track. I like Meb's chances in that situation.

After I finished, I was whisked away to drug testing by officials. No victory lap. No draping myself in the flag. No interview with NBC afterward, nor did I get a follow-up the next day on the *Today* show as had been customary for U.S. medalists during the Games. I got my kicks from teammates, though. Alan congratulated me by placing me in a bear hug and picking me up. Dan, not surprised by my medal, told NBC's Marty Liquori that "Meb's the toughest guy I know."

At the finish in the old stadium, David Monti, the elite athlete coordinator for the New York City Marathon, told me, "Congratulations. . . . Did you know you were 34 seconds from $500,000?" The New York and Chicago marathons had

This photo of me was taken after my family made it to Italy. Look at my curly hair!

We lost a lot of family photos when we left Eritrea, so I value this one of my dad as a young man. People say I look like him in his younger years. ▼

EARLY YEARS

I loved running for San Diego High School. This photo was taken when I was just an underclassman, but I was already eager to get out in front.

Coach Bob Larsen and I were recognized at a UCLA basketball game in Pauley Pavilion for my collegiate performances. Coach has been a great mentor in my life.

My family was by my side when I graduated from UCLA . . . ▼

◀ . . . and so were my friends, mentors, and lifelong advisers Steve and Gail Van Camp. I wouldn't be where I am today without them.

This is a dream training situation, with great partners. Running with others motivates us all to do our best. ▲

Here I am with one of my heroes— marathon legend Joan Benoit Samuelson. ▶

Even though Ryan Hall, Khalid Khannouchi, and I are often competitors, I'm fortunate that I can also call these guys my friends. ▲

One of the many benefits to living and training in a great climate—icing my body in a natural creek instead of in a tub. The ice bath after a hard run is my God time when I am alone. ▶

Proudly holding both U.S. and Eritrean flags after making my first Olympic team in 2000—representing two very important parts of who I am.

MEMORABLE MOMENTS

Posing in a PowerBar ad with two cool guys—Olympian Dan Browne and Josh Cox, whom I've known since high school. In high school, Josh's late father used to always tell Josh to "stay with Mebrahtom," even when he was ahead of me.

Receiving the silver medal at the 2004 Olympic Games was one of the crowning moments of my life. (Later I gave the flowers I'm holding to Yordanos on our first official date.)

Celebrating at dinner with Yordanos after I popped the question in front of a Zales in New York City.

In my family, we honor our two cultures with a two-day wedding celebration. First, a tuxedo-and-gown ceremony for anywhere up to 1,000 people . . .

. . . followed by a traditional Eritrean reception the next day. By these standards, our 475-person wedding was actually small!

At this press conference with Abdi Abdirahman and Ryan Shay, no one had any idea that we would lose Ryan so soon. Ryan was a great young man.

I've been blessed to travel all over the world for different races. Here I'm exploring London with Merhawi (my brother and manager), Yordanos, and Sara before the London Marathon in 2007. ▼

FRIENDS & FAMILY

ERITREA

▲ My cousin Mussie Kiflu and I on a visit to the Eritrean village of Adi Gombolo, one of the places where I grew up.

◄ I wore my silver medal to show my relatives, but was touched to find that it didn't mean as much to them as I'd thought. It was me they wanted to hear about and spend time with.

Standing at my grandfather's grave, I ▶ remembered how even after he lost his sight, he would proudly feel the muscles in my "magic legs."

◄ In 2005, I was honored by the Eritrean Development Foundation. Here I am with Girma Asmerom, the former Eritrean ambassador to the United States, and Alphonso Jackson, then secretary of Housing and Urban Development for President Bush. EDF was able to raise over $170,000 that evening.

Donating shoes to Eritrean running club coaches on behalf of the Eritrean American Athletics Association (EAAA) with my fellow representative Kiflay Habte.

Growing up in Eritrea, I didn't even know that running was a sport. When I run there now, it feels like I've come full circle. My cousin Kudus caught me in action in Adi Beyani. Not bad for one of his first-ever photos.

Yordanos and our Eritrean host doing laundry—and having fun—together.

My parents have always been proud of me . . . but everyone knows they're the true champions in our family.

VICTORY

I always set out my gear the night before a marathon—the 2009 New York City Marathon was no exception—but I don't always put my bib on a pillow! Just a goofy mood, I guess.

I was celebrating my strong lead in 2009 as I neared the finish line, but I didn't fully believe it was happening until I felt that tape break across the big "USA" on my chest.

I was so nervous reading the Top 10 list on the *Late Show With David Letterman* after winning the race, but it was a huge honor!

© 2009 Worldwide Pants Incorporated. All Rights Reserved.

The most important people in my life: Yordanos, Fiyori, Sara, and Yohana.

put up a $500,000 bonus for any American winner. I did, however, receive built-in bonuses from Nike and the NYRR. But I wasn't thinking about the money. All this started because of a seventh grade PE class mile run that turned into a passion. I had wanted an "A, E" at Roosevelt Junior High and hoped I had earned the same marks in Athens.

From the old stadium we were driven with police escort to the main Olympic Stadium for the medal ceremony and a press conference. A lot of friends and family have told me I looked somber on the medal stand. I was intent on being respectful, mindful of conduct by some U.S. sprinters in 2000 that caused controversy.

Trust me, I was happy, both for myself and for U.S. distance running. I had earned the first U.S. medal in the men's marathon since Frank Shorter's silver in 1976, which followed his gold in 1972. In addition, four years after the low point of Sydney—with just one man and one woman in the marathon—the United States was the only country in the world with a medalist in each marathon. Not Kenya, not Ethiopia, not Japan. Just the good ol' USA. And to think that Deena and I were both from Mammoth Lakes—a town with about five stoplights had two marathon medalists. Mammoth Lakes mayor Rick Wood declared August 22 and August 29 Deena and Meb days, respectively. When I finally made it back to San Diego two weeks after the race, over 200 friends and family members, along with the media, met me at the airport. A limousine took me to a community celebration.

It had been another high point in Athens, though nothing could surpass the feeling from 18 years earlier when the family was reunited after five years apart. Back then my father didn't recognize me because I was so small and malnourished. Now I was an Olympic silver medalist. Reflecting on my family's journey, I was humbled and grateful.

If I felt shortchanged on attention at the old Olympic Stadium, the feeling faded in the new stadium. Our medal ceremony was the start of the closing ceremonies, which was broadcast to millions around the world. Thousands of athletes and more than 100,000 fans had gathered for the finale of the XXVIII Olympiad as night fell.

During all the post-race confusion, I lost the laurel wreath I had removed from my head and placed aside. Thankfully, I still had the flowers I was given on the medal stand. I headed back to the American College dormitories to pack and catch an early-morning flight. There was a young woman I wanted to impress in Tampa. I thought the flowers from Athens would be a nice touch for our first date.

RUNNER'S TIP

When doing repeats or a regular run, try to run faster at the end of the workout. That simulates what you're trying to do in races and should help your finishes.

OVERCOMER'S TIP

Accomplish something every day and give thanks for the ability to do it.

7.0 / **LOVE STORY**

FOR YEARS I HAD BEEN SEEKING but not finding a special woman. Looking back at my journals, you could tell it was a concern. There were entries, often as part of yearly goals, such as "Find a girlfriend," "Have a long-term relationship," "Be engaged by 2001–2002."

That wasn't happening. I found the frustrations of my search for "the one" spilling over into my conversations with two of my most important mentors: Bob Larsen and Steve Van Camp. Coach Larsen would tell me I should expand the field, maybe look beyond the Eritrean community. Steve would tell me, "In God's good time, Meb, not yours." Steve gave me a question to ask myself if I had found the right woman: Can you imagine that woman raising your children?

My mother was always praying for me. She worried that I was naive and gullible, that girls would exploit me. Gail Van Camp also asked God to direct me in my search. One time during college, after I had explained my dating frustrations to her, we prayed together that I'd find someone special. My father always told us that a good wife is a gift from God.

I had had girlfriends. Kiesha Porter and I had dated in high school and college. Like me, she was a track athlete, a hurdler/jumper who went to UCLA. She comes from a great family that gets along with mine—I have even prayed with her parents. However, I eventually realized that both my family and I would be most comfortable if I married a woman of Eritrean background. Although cultural differences stood in the way of long-term involvement with Kiesha, she is a wonderful person, and we remain close friends.

In the summer of 2004, I attended an Eritrean soccer tournament in San Jose. This annual event, which rotates locations, is really more about culture and friendships than it is about soccer, though the competition is fierce. My older brothers, Fitsum and Aklilu, have played in it. One of my post-professional running goals is to play in it myself.

That July, I was there as a spectator, taking a breather from hard training after I had qualified for the Athens Olympic team in the marathon and before I qualified in the 10,000 at the track & field trials later in the month in Sacramento. For me, it was a chance to party. Now keep in mind that partying for me does not involve alcohol or drugs. If I'm carrying a cup, it's filled with water or juice. But as I've mentioned, I do love dancing to Eritrean music into the wee hours. The way I look at it, it's like a morning run. Additionally, I had been invited to the tournament to be part of a panel of young, successful Eritreans who would speak to interested children and teens. So between the opportunity to give back to the youth, dance to the music of the biggest Eritrean singers, and watch my brother Aklilu play soccer, I decided to fit the tournament into my schedule.

On the opening day, I was watching a game when a guy accompanied by several women sat down near me. I couldn't keep my eyes off one of the women. Not only was she good-looking and well dressed, but I liked her manner. She carried herself well and seemed friendly, greeting anyone who approached her group. Bells were ringing inside of me. Of course, I did not say one word to her.

But I started doing research. The next day I bumped into the guy she had been sitting with. We talked a little bit, and then I said, "Who was that girl sitting with you yesterday? If she's your girlfriend, congratulations. If she's your sister, I'm sorry. If she's single, I'd like to meet her."

"What's she look like?" he asked.

"She's light skinned with long hair."

Right away he knew who I was talking about. "Yordanos."

He made a couple of phone calls and found out she was at the game watching her brother Marikos play. When we found her, the sun was setting. I needed to make a move as soon as the game ended. I was nervously thinking, *How am I going to do this? God help me.* It was like my self-talk during a tough part of a race—I was scared to approach her. Finally, I figured, *What's the worst thing that could happen? Might as well go for it.*

So I went up to her and started chatting. "What brings you here?" I asked. She told me that her brother Marikos was playing and that they were having a family vacation. She asked me what I was doing. I told her my brother was playing too. I explained that I had a big track meet coming up but that I'd already made the Olympic team in the marathon.

As it turned out, the fact that I was a serious runner went right over her head. This embarrasses her to this day. She thought I was some recreational runner and all she heard was "marathon." She immediately introduced me to her sister-in-law, Lettie, who had run marathons. So right away I was pushed off to the sister-in-law, who asked me which marathons I'd run. Then she asked me about my family and how long we had been in the United States. As it turns out, Lettie was screening me for Yordanos!

Afterward she told Yordanos, "He's a special guy, and you're going to marry him." At the time, I was just trying to confirm that Yordanos was single because, if so, I wanted her phone number. As we were all leaving the game, Yordanos asked if I was going to the party that night. I told her no because I had an important tempo run to do Saturday morning and needed sleep Friday night. She said, "Come on, man, I run, too. When everybody's sleeping at my hotel, I'm on the treadmill." She had no clue what kind of runner I was, what I was aiming for, and how seriously I needed to train. Yet I couldn't have cared less. Before we left the game, I introduced her to my brother Fitsum and a couple of my sisters. There I was—I barely knew her and was already introducing her to my family.

My instincts soon kicked in. I wound up going to the party because I realized Yordanos was somebody special. The only trouble was, there were about a thousand people at the party. I finally spotted her, talking to a guy who was trying to hit on her. I became uncharacteristically aggressive. I stepped in and said, "You're dancing with me." During our first dance, I took one look in her eyes and thought, *This is it. She is a special girl.*

If she's single—I still have to find out for sure—then she could be the one. We danced a few more times.

It turned out Yordanos was having similar thoughts. She told me later she remembers thinking, *This guy could be my husband.*

YORDANOS ASGEDOM: I'm glad Meb came to that party because that's when he won my heart. He kept talking about his family. You could tell his passion for them. For both of us, our families are our priority. I thought, *This is a really cool guy. I like him.*

We arranged to meet at another party the next night, where we had a good time talking again. As we were leaving, I suggested we go on a date in the near future. My heart broke when she said, "I'm flying out tomorrow morning." I thought I had met a California girl. But she lived in Tampa and had to work Monday. I was crushed. I had recently ended a relationship that wasn't working, in part because it was long distance.

Still, I got Yordanos's e-mail address and cell phone number. She had misplaced her cell phone and couldn't punch in my number. So someone got one of those Starbucks cardboard coffee cup sleeves and another person gave me a pen. I scribbled down my number and e-mail. I told her this was information that I didn't want her to lose.

A day or two later, Yordanos e-mailed me. Then she left me a voice mail saying that she had a good time in San Jose and meeting me had made it extra special. I called Merhawi, who was in England on a law school study-abroad program, to tell him, "I think I've found the one." I told Fitsum, I told my training partners, and I told other friends the same thing. I was so excited, but they were telling me to calm down. "You just met this woman, and now you're talking about marrying her?"

YORDANOS ASGEDOM: The more I talked to Meb, the more I felt like I was talking to someone who was an exact reflection of my values, who I am, and what I stand for. It was friendship at first, but the more we talked, it was hard to resist falling in love. I was making excuses for not having a relationship because I didn't want to deal with the long-distance aspect. But you can't fight that, especially when you hear a voice that is echoing.

I prayed really hard about it. I said, "Lord, I don't want to break what you have for me. I remember I prayed at the beginning of the year for something special." I decided I wasn't going to mess it up just because my mind was thinking a long-distance relationship wasn't practical. I felt we had a special chemistry, and I was going to commit to making it work.

Yordanos and I began a telecommunications courtship. We talked, texted, or e-mailed each other pretty much every day. Sometimes the exchanges were short, and sometimes they were long. There were phone calls until 3:00 a.m.—her time. Hey, I still needed to get my sleep. We were getting to know each other despite being 3,000 miles apart.

Yordanos began to understand the level of my running

when she watched the 10,000 race at the trials on TV. I dominated the race and won. Later she told me she felt like an idiot for all the comments she'd made to me before about running. Knowing she would be watching was an inspiration to me. I wanted to put on a show. Some of her brothers were aware of who I was and began to fill her in.

In one of our talks shortly after that I told her, "I'm not into playing games. I think you're a special person. If your heart is in this, let's continue. If it's not, we can just be friends." Of course, it would have destroyed me if she had wanted to bail out.

The relationship continued long distance. I invited Yordanos to come to Mammoth Lakes where I was training, explaining that I needed to run at altitude and couldn't visit her. The Eritrean custom is that the guy has to visit first, and she wanted to adhere to that. I also suggested that she come to Athens, which she considered but ultimately turned down.

I told her, "I have a big stage waiting for me in Athens, but right after that I'm coming to visit you."

YORDANOS ASGEDOM: I came very close to going to Athens. Not going is one of the things I'll regret for the rest of my life. Meb would never admit it, but I think he felt lonely there after winning the medal. That's what I saw in his face. If there had been another family member there for him to share the moment with, it would have been different. Family is everything to him, and nobody was there. I could have been. I have a guilty conscience over that. We as a family feel terrible that nobody close was there for him.

And that's what I did after earning the silver medal in the closing event of the Olympics. Knowing how important family was to me, Yordanos begged me to return to San Diego first to be with my family before coming to Tampa.

It meant a lot to me that Yordanos thought of my family first and wanted me to go to San Diego. That showed how considerate she was and how aware she was of the importance of family. But I was adamant about going to Tampa. I told her, "I am honored to have the silver medal, but that does not change who I am. I made plans to see you right after the Games, and that's what I'm going to do. I'm a man of my word."

///////////////////

It was a fun trip from Athens to Tampa, even though I didn't sleep after the race. When I got to the Athens airport for the team's 4:50 a.m. charter flight to Frankfurt, I received a standing ovation from the athletes. That felt great. During a layover in Frankfurt, Elva Dryer and Kate O'Neill, members of the U.S. team in the 10,000, tried to talk United Airlines into giving me an upgrade to first class, but there were no vacant seats. One of the flight attendants asked if she could have the medal ceremony flowers. I told her she could until we got to the States. She put the flowers in a vase to keep them fresh.

I presented the bouquet to Yordanos when I landed. She told me she was impressed even though she describes herself as "not a candy-and-flowers girl." Actually, we were on the same wavelength: she had flowers for me. On the way to her home, we stopped at the Olive Garden restaurant—our first date. And the meal was on the house when the manager recognized me and found out about the occasion.

The flowers scored some points, but what may have sealed the deal in the relationship were some of our discussions about faith and my gift of *tsebel*, which I carry with me as a reminder of God's power. She was impressed because faith is important to her and her family, just as it is to mine.

Our families have a lot in common. Yordanos is one of 10 children. She lived in a village in Eritrea that had no electricity or running water. Her parents came to the United States in May 1983. Before that, her father went to Sudan, where he was later joined by the rest of the family. (Many Eritreans in the United States have similar stories. My brothers and sisters get teased by relatives for having taken an easy route—we flew out of Eritrea. Some of them walked and rode camels to get to Sudan.) Most of Yordanos's brothers and sisters have graduated from college.

Our relationship soon hit fast-forward. We shared close families, strong religious beliefs, and ambition. Yordanos was the assistant vice president of a Bank of America branch and specialized in premier clients.

She came to San Diego for Thanksgiving and met my family and friends. I had previously shown a picture of Yordanos to my second mother, Amoy Letemichael, who told me, "Do not let her go." My mother told me that Yordanos was the best thing to ever happen to me. Yordanos and I got engaged in May 2005 and married that November.

Because family is important to us, we flew in several of my West Coast family members and relatives, especially on my mom's side, for the wedding in Tampa. We wanted to set a good example for some of the younger kids regarding Eritrean marriage customs. "I can't imagine them not being able to see the ceremony," Yordanos said. We also decided to have the reception catered so the family would not be overworked in cooking for everyone.

Eritrean weddings are large and long, by American standards. Back in Eritrea they are villagewide celebrations that can go for six days. The U.S. version has been cut to two days, in concession to work and travel schedules. Our 475 guests did not constitute a particularly large wedding. About 1,000 people attended Fitsum's wedding and more than that attended my sister Bahghi's wedding in San Diego. My father is a big reason for an expansive guest list. He'll look at it and say, "You can't invite this person and not invite these people. How will it look in church the next time we see them?" My dad has been invited to a lot of weddings, so the culture dictates reciprocity. In order to cut expenses, we skipped an engagement party because our priority was getting family to the wedding.

Our guests also included several members of the running community, including New York City Marathon director Mary Wittenberg. At the reception, guests Alan Culpepper and his wife, Shayne—both Olympians—tried some Eritrean dancing. Later Alan told me, "Now I see why you're always in shape."

//////////////

Yordanos and I soon had a growing family in Mammoth Lakes. Sara, the first of our three daughters, was born in 2006. Fiyori was born in 2008, and Yohana came along in 2010. Thankfully, all of the deliveries were safe and the babies healthy. The biggest decision we had to make with the girls was how to name them. We wanted to maintain Eritrean customs, where children take on the name of the father. That had not happened to me or my siblings because of a misunderstanding and dispute with immigration and Catholic officials in Italy. My father's first name, Russom, should have been the last name of all his children. Instead we were named Keflezighi, the name of his grandfather and my great-grandfather.

At a family meeting, we decided to honor my father by giving all of his grandchildren the last name of Russom. So our daughters are Sara, Fiyori, and Yohana Russom. If they had been born in Eritrea, they'd be Sara, Fiyori, and Yohana Mebrahtom. Instead, following another Eritrean custom, my name is the middle name for each of my daughters. The only trouble comes when we travel as a family. I'm Mebrahtom Russom Sef Keflezighi and my wife is Yordanos Asgedom. (She has followed the Eritrean tradition of keeping her family name after marriage.) Our children don't share either name. We always carry birth certificates and our marriage license to help sort things out with airport security the best we can.

Thankfully, I have an understanding wife to help negotiate life's problems, large and small. Without Yordanos, I would be like a car with a flat tire. As beautiful as she is on the outside, Yordanos is even more beautiful inside. She cares about family and me as an individual. If I never ran another step, it wouldn't matter to her.

At the same time, she is my biggest encourager. She texts me Scripture and frequently reminds me that "with God all things are possible" (Matthew 19:26, NIV), a favorite passage of ours. On those Saturdays when my family and I are in San Diego, we attend the Eritrean Orthodox Church, where we are members. When we're in Mammoth Lakes, Yordanos and the girls join me for services at a church in town after I've finished that day's long run. Together we are trying to pass on our faith and thankfulness for God's blessings to our three daughters.

My family loves Yordanos, and she loves them. Since we live in California and see my family often, we usually head to Florida when I take training breaks after a marathon so we can spend time with her side of the family.

GAIL VAN CAMP: Yordanos was instantly likable. She's down-to-earth, completely unpretentious, totally honest. She's very positive without being a Pollyanna. She's genuine in her personality and genuine in her faith. She's the woman we were all praying for Meb to meet.

I don't think I could function without Yordanos. She's very smart. She handles all the bills and family paperwork. She doesn't want me to worry about anything that is unnecessary. She's a businesswoman who bounces ideas about my career back and forth with Merhawi, my brother and agent. They screen deals for me.

When we met, Yordanos was assistant vice president of a bank in Tampa. Now she's sacrificing her own career to help my athletic career and raise our children. We believed it would be best to have at least one parent at home while raising the kids. That's what our parents did for us. If one of the girls awakens at night, it's Yordanos who responds. She wants me to get sleep. Same with afternoon naps between workouts. Even when she was pregnant and tired herself,

Yordanos made sure I got a nap if I needed it on a tough workout day. As a marathon nears, I'll often head downstairs to sleep so I'm not disturbed if the girls wake up in the middle of the night.

Yordanos doesn't complain. She's incredibly unselfish. "You need your rest," she tells me. "I'm not trying to compete to be the best runner in the world."

We laugh now that it must have been destiny that we met. When she was managing portfolios for individual investors at Bank of America, Yordanos was a workaholic. For years, she refused to take a vacation, despite her family's urging. Finally she relented in 2004 and, after a short stay in Los Angeles, decided to extend her trip a few more days to attend the soccer tournament in San Jose. Now that she knows the realities of competition at the world-class level and understands my work ethic, she can't believe that I changed plans on a Friday night to attend a party when I had an important workout the next day. (By the way, I finished that 25-minute tempo run.)

The funny thing is that some people expected that marrying and starting a family would be a detriment to my career. The opposite has happened. I'm more motivated than ever to train and compete. My family isn't a distraction, thanks to all the efforts of Yordanos. In return, I want to do my best for Yordanos and our daughters. I'd like to win them all a special medal.

When I mentioned to Aba Teklezighi, the priest who married us, that I thought marriage was like a marathon, he agreed and said that Yordanos and I modeled that well. Marriage requires patience and the willingness to remain committed during both good and bad times.

What's most comforting is that I know Yordanos's love does not depend on my performance. She provides unconditional love and support, something I would need in the coming years.

RUNNER'S TIP

I try to carry a snack bag, kind of a nutritional first-aid kit. I like to refuel throughout the day on healthy stuff. My bag usually contains a PowerBar plus apples, bananas, raisins, and dates. I always have water available.

OVERCOMER'S TIP

Instead of rushing to make things happen, rely on God's perfect timing.

8.0 / LIFE ON THE RUN: THE ELITE GAME

WHEN I WAS A ROOKIE PRO RUNNER in August 1998 and in Brussels for a 10,000, I was thrilled to get an invitation from superstar Paul Tergat. He suggested we have tea and a chat in our hotel coffee shop. The way he welcomed me was a typically warm East African gesture that I will always cherish. I liked that he put his arm around me and called me "my American friend."

Tergat was the kind of runner I aspired to be. The Kenyan was in the midst of winning five world cross country titles. He was coming off an epic 10,000 duel with Ethiopia's Haile Gebrselassie in the 1996 Atlanta Olympics. He was bright, a businessman who wanted to help grow his country's economy, and caring, a philanthropist who was interested in eradicating hunger in Africa.

But what I, only 23 years old at the time, most wanted to learn that afternoon from the 29-year-old superstar was what workouts he was doing. "I want to get to where you are, so

I need to be doing what you are doing," I said. He chuckled before giving me some great advice: be patient.

Tergat knew from experience that I needed years to develop. The former Kenyan basketball player-turned-runner explained that when he started running at the age of 21 after joining the military, he couldn't do the workouts he was currently doing. "Put in the time," he told me. "You've got to gradually increase your training. You are not at the level I am. I could give you my workouts, and you might be able to hang with me for a day or a week, but eventually you would break down if you had not done the preparation. But if you do things right and work hard, you will get there."

Then he went out and lapped his American friend to win in 26:46.44. I finished 16th in 28:31.14. Tergat was well under 27 minutes; I wasn't close to breaking 28. He was 1:45, or more than a lap and a half, ahead of me. I had a lot of ground to make up and a lot of work ahead of me, but I wasn't demoralized. Who could ever have guessed that six years later we'd both be marathoners and that I would beat him on the way to a silver medal in the Athens Games?

Whenever people ask me for running advice, I tell them what Tergat told me. Improve your training gradually. Be realistic. Set attainable goals, achieve them, then reset them. I was fortunate with my coaches—Eduardo Ramos at San Diego High School, world-class marathoner Ron Tabb during my high school off-seasons, and Bob Larsen, who has been with me ever since I entered UCLA in 1994. They brought me along slowly, emphasizing quality over quantity in training.

In my first two years of running at San Diego High School, I averaged about 25 to 35 miles per week. I went to 35 to 40 miles as a junior and 40 to 50 miles as a senior. The most I ever ran in one week in high school was 56 miles, which I did just one time. I went from a good local runner as a freshman to a state and national champion as a senior.

At UCLA, I averaged between 50 and 65 miles a week as a freshman and sophomore; 60 to 75 as a junior; and 80 to 85 as a senior. I was an All-American in track and cross country as a freshman but didn't win NCAA titles until my junior and senior years. By the time I met with Tergat in 1998, I had had maybe one 100-mile week in my life.

Now I'll hit a maximum of about 130 to 135 miles per week during a heavy phase of marathon training. Those are done mainly at altitude, translating to roughly 143 to 145 miles at sea level. What some casual runners usually don't understand is how demanding the training is for an elite distance runner. "Do you run every day?" is a question I'm often asked. There may be as many as 12 running sessions per week. When you finish one workout, you're immediately trying to recover to get ready for the next one.

A typical marathon buildup week starts on Monday—an easy day—with a single 10- to 12-mile run. It used to always be 12 for me, but now that I'm getting older, I realize one fewer mile may be better than one more mile. The run is followed by a 15-minute ice bath—I often go to a nearby creek for these—to help my legs recover. I take the afternoon off from running because I need to recover from the previous day's long run: 36-plus miles within 24 hours would be too much to take. Later in the day, we head to Snowcreek Athletic Club for a gym session that includes core and flexibility exercises, weightlifting, and plyometrics—exercises to increase explosiveness.

Tuesday is a day for repeats. The session might consist of three or four two-mile repeats. At an altitude of 4,000 feet I've averaged sub-9 minutes with a three-minute rest between repeats. Sometimes we'll go up to 9,000 feet, where just walking can take the air out of your lungs. We have a 2.2-mile loop around Lake Mary. I may do those as fast as 10:19 with a four- to five-minute recovery. Another staple: 8 x 1 mile repeats with two-minute recoveries. When I can get through this workout feeling pretty good on the heels of the Sunday long run, I know I'm in good shape. With a three-mile warm-up beforehand and a three-mile cooldown afterward, plus drills and stretching, the session can last up to three hours—not counting the drive time to and from the site. There's the mandatory icing after every morning run as well.

After lunch and a quick nap, I'll run 30 to 45 minutes. Then there's the gym session at the Snowcreek Athletic Club, which can be the longest workout of the day. Usually I'm home by 6:30 p.m., but sometimes it's closer to 7:30. Sara, Fiyori, and Yohana usually have eaten by then. I'll grab a bite, put the girls to bed, and then read to them until they fall asleep. Many of their books were gifts from Dave Johnston, one of my high school teachers who has become a good friend.

Wednesday is a semi-long day. It consists of 16 to 21 miles simulating a marathon build-up with the last five miles getting progressively faster. There's no afternoon run, but there is a gym session—we hit the gym every day of the week except Sunday. If I'm feeling energetic, I might hop on my mountain bike to save my joints and ride for an hour or so at 9,000 feet.

Thursday is another easy day. I'll usually put in 10 miles in the morning. The pace depends on how I feel—I don't push

it. If it's summer and the snow has cleared at the higher eleva-
tions, I'll do the run at 9,000 feet. Toward the end of the run
I'm usually going faster than a six-minute-per-mile pace. In
the afternoon, I'll go for 30 minutes or so. Sometimes I'll ice
my legs after both runs. That's a total of 30 minutes in cold
water up to my waist—not fun. If I'm icing at home in 50-
to 55-degree water, Yordanos will bring me warm milk with
honey to help me get through the ordeal.

The icing is important because I need my legs recovered
for Friday, which is my bread-and-butter day. There's always
a little anxiety for this workout. It's a tempo run, which is
comfortably difficult. For me that is a sub-5-minute pace that
could go as low as 4:36 on a downhill stretch. Depending on
where I am in my training, the distance will vary from 5 to 15
miles, usually at 7,000 feet. Before a marathon, I like to have
two or three 15-mile tempos under my belt. The Tuesday and
Friday workouts are good indicators of my fitness and also
build my confidence.

The tempo runs are preceded by a three-mile warm-up
run followed by a half mile of strides in 100-meter segments.
They're followed by a three-mile cooldown. So if the tempo is
15 miles, the total mileage for the session is 21.5 miles.

The afternoon session is four to seven miles, depending on
how I'm feeling. The total mileage for the day often exceeds
the 26.2-mile length of the marathon. If I'm feeling good, I
sometimes get the urge to extend the tempo run to 16 miles,
but I usually resist. Instead, I run the last mile a bit faster. It's
important to leave a workout thinking, *Hey, I can do a little
more,* rather than completely trashing yourself.

Saturday is also an easy day. There's a 10- to 12-miler in

the morning. There may be a 30-minute run in the afternoon, depending on what's called for in the Sunday workout. If it's a super-long run the next day, I'll take the afternoon off to get more rest.

Sundays traditionally are the long run day. If I'm in an early phase of marathon training, that means a 20-miler. Later in the training block, I'll go as far as 26 or 28 miles. I may start the run as slowly as 6:30 to 7:00 per mile as I ease into things, and by the end I'm running 5:30s or 5:40s. I'd rather be slower at the beginning and faster at the end. And then I do it all over again the following week, ideally for at least 10 weeks leading up to a marathon. The last long Sunday run comes three weeks before the race.

If you're doing that much running, nutrition is crucial. I need 4,000 to 5,000 calories daily, which is a lot for a 123-pounder. My general strategy is to try to eat two main meals and then do a lot of grazing throughout the day.

For a pre-run breakfast, it's usually *himbasha*, a traditional Eritrean bread that is a great source of carbohydrates, or a bagel that I top with honey. Both Yordanos and my mother make delicious versions of *himbasha*. My parents used to send me batches by FedEx when I was at UCLA. Our friends Ryan and Sara Hall sometimes pick up a supply of *himbasha* for themselves—sharing is caring. Andrew and Deena Kastor are big fans of *himbasha* as well.

Within 15 minutes of completing the morning workout, I drink a bottle of Generation UCAN, a sports drink, and eat a portion of a PowerBar—two of the products I endorse. Once I get home, I eat the first of my larger meals. If it's a hard day, I usually have an omelet or an egg sandwich with *himbasha*. If it's an easy day, I have a turkey sandwich. I try to add as many fruits as possible as well.

If possible, I take a nap. Before I leave for the afternoon session, I have the rest of the PowerBar. After the afternoon run and before a gym session, it's time for another PowerBar and fruit.

For dinner on a hard day, I have steak or another protein source, along with salad, veggies, and a baked potato. I eat a lot of greens—especially broccoli and peppers. The night before tempos and long runs, I stick with carbohydrates—pasta or rice—like I would before a marathon. Some nights just before bedtime, I have *himbasha*, especially if it's fresh and hot, with a glass of organic milk, since my bone density is a concern.

I've been a competitive runner since I went out for cross country in 1990 at San Diego High School, And I've been keeping a detailed training log—another staple for a serious runner—since 1993. I still use the same forms given to me by Coach Manny Batista, who organized summer running camps when I was in high school. By the summer of 2010, I had logged 53,370.5 miles—more than two times around the world!

If you're going to push your body through demanding weeks that result in mega mileage over the years, you need help and helpers. That's why I like the quote from Wilma Rudolph, a sprinter who won three gold medals in the 1960 Olympics: "No matter what accomplishments you make, somebody helps you."

Many of my runs are done with pacers on a bike, who provide me with company and drinks. I've had a number through the years: Rich Levy, whom I've known since I was in high school competing against his son, David; Mario Arce, whose brother, Antonio, was one of my high school rivals; Dirk Addis; and Bejan Abiahi. Mario was with me every step of the way from 2004 to preparations for the marathon Olympic trials in 2007. Dirk helped me prior to New York in 2009 and Boston in 2010. Bejan helped pace me on a bike and ran with me on easy days through my injury rehabilitation in Colorado Springs in 2008. In recent years, I've also received lots of help from Tomas Rodriguez. Rita Klabacha, an exercise physiologist for the Mammoth Track Club, has biked with me as well.

Rich has been an influence since high school. He has always told me that you have to have fun with running to keep doing it. He used to drive David and me to Balboa Park, Mission Bay Park, and Del Mar for training runs. He's retired in San Diego now, but he always reminds me, "Hey, I'm just a phone call away." He'll come up to Mammoth Lakes on a moment's notice and stay with me if I need him. It's not all work and no play with Rich, though. He'll take me sailing or we'll go out kayaking. Sometimes I fall asleep in the rear of the two-person kayak while Rich does all the paddling. I can hear people thinking out loud, "What's wrong with this picture? The old guy is doing all the work and the young guy is sleeping." But Rich knows that I can't do too much paddling because if my upper body bulks up, it will compromise my running.

I don't think I could do all the mileage without the help of my pacers. It would be too difficult mentally and also too scary. Running in isolated areas around Mammoth, I'm afraid of encountering wild animals. Yes, the guy born in Africa worries about mountain lions and bears. I have a fear of being attacked from behind by a mountain lion; I'm always looking behind me. I've had more experience than I want to with bears, which have broken into my car, trash cans, and house. I'm scared of dogs, which seem to randomly attack me. In addition to the attack by the German shepherd on the training run right before the 2004 Olympics, I was forced to miss the 2005 London Marathon when I strained an Achilles tendon backpedaling in training to avoid another dog attack.

Another component in keeping me healthy are the regular ice baths. Although they are a painful step, ice baths are extremely effective at reducing inflammation, muscle strains, and soreness. I'm so convinced of that, I always travel with a thermometer to be sure the water I'm soaking in is the correct 50 to 55 degrees.

If I can't use the creeks around Mammoth Lakes, I buy large bags of ice at the grocery store to put in the bathtub at home. When I walk out of a store with 40 pounds of ice, people tend to ask, "Where's the party?" Believe me, an ice bath is no party. But as marathoner Deena Kastor says, the toughest parts are the first three minutes and the first three days.

I use the ice baths as Scripture time. I'll read the Bible or some other religious books. (Recently, I've been reading Philip Yancey's devotional *Grace Notes*, a gift from Ryan Hall and his wife, Sara.) Because I spend these 15 minutes alone, they're a natural time to reach out to God and talk with Him.

Another book I frequently read during my ice baths is Bruce Wilkinson's *The Prayer of Jabez*. The Bible says the Hebrew name Jabez means "painful," because Jabez's birth caused his mother so much pain. Since my mom went through agony with me during childbirth, I feel some sort of kinship with Jabez. Wilkinson's best-selling book is based on 1 Chronicles 4:9-10, where Jabez's prayer is recorded. In his prayer, Jabez asks the Lord to bless him and increase his territory. That's a plea I can relate to. When I'm competing, I often tell God that if it's His will that I finish second or third, I'm okay with that—but I'd love to win! I also resonate with the end of Jabez's prayer: "Please be with me in all that I do, and keep me from all trouble and pain!" (verse 10). I certainly sense God's presence and power as I run through the mountains of Mammoth Lakes, but the ice baths that follow can be agonizing.

While ice baths are usually done in solitude, other recovery therapies require others' expertise. They include stretching, massage, other soft tissue work, and body alignment. I usually get worked on three times a week—Tuesday, Friday, and Sunday, after the key runs of the week. The timing is strategic. I like deep tissue work to flush out the waste products, and I don't want sore legs from the treatments to interfere with the week's toughest workouts.

I rely on a huge support network to get the most out of myself. It takes a village to succeed in all aspects of life, and staying healthy is the key to achieving athletic goals. At my main training base in Mammoth Lakes, the Sierra Park Orthopedic and Rehabilitation Therapy (SPORT) center staff, along with Gary Oschman, Andrew Kastor (Deena's husband), and Jennifer Lane, have been great. In San Diego, I use the services of the La Jolla Physical Therapy Center staff. Robb Latimer and Kevin McCarey provide massage; Gino Cinco and Dr. Shawn Robek are Active Release Technique (ART) practitioners there. And I've gone to Dr. Craig Van Otten in Fremont for his ART service. Dr. Van Otten charges a minimal amount because he says it is an honor to help elite athletes maximize their potential.

Devin Young, an ART student, helped me prepare for the 2010 Boston Marathon when the knee issue arose.

In Tampa, where I head after most marathons, I see Dr. Michael Eggleston for massage and Tommy Rhee for ART. In New York, there are Jim Wharton and Jimmy Lynch, the mayor of the New York running community. Jim Wharton's son, Phil, who's based in Flagstaff, Arizona, is at many running events and helps me on the road. Dr. Justin Whittaker travels to big races to work on me and my Mammoth Track Club teammates. We are lucky to have Terrence Mahon, who does therapy in trigger points and balance.

For medical purposes I've gotten good advice the past couple of years from Dr. Lewis Maharam in New York City, who specializes in sports medicine and is the former medical director of the New York City Marathon. I don't think you can achieve or stay at world-class level unless you have great medical support. The training is too demanding and the injuries are so inevitable that you need knowledgeable people working on your body and advising you. I seek advice from a lot of sources and interpret it the best I can.

///////////////////////

Some runners use performance-enhancing drugs to help their performance. It's a sad reality of not only road racing and track, but of all sports these days. For some distance runners, it's tempting to use steroids or erythropoietin (EPO). Steroids, derivatives of the male sex hormone testosterone, speed muscle recovery and usually are associated with bulging muscles. A marathoner on steroids wouldn't bulk up, but could run a lot more miles. EPO, a synthetic hormone, increases red blood cells, which carry oxygen and prolong a person's endurance. I increase my red blood cells the old-fashioned way—by training at altitude.

I've never come close to being tempted by these drugs, but I have been approached. It's been subtle. Nobody has walked up to me with a bunch of pills and said, "Here, take these. You'll lower your PR by two minutes." But people in the sport—I'm not going to name them—have said things like, "There are doctors we have who can help you," or, "There are things we can do with your blood to help you." The clear implication is that they can provide banned drugs and/or suggest strategies to beat the testing system.

I've never been interested. It would be too contradictory to my background. The biggest deterrent of drug use to me is not the two-year ban for a positive test—it's the dishonor a drug violation would bring to me and my family. My parents have always taught me and my siblings that there's a right way and a wrong way of doing things and that God knows which way you choose. I just couldn't carry the burden of bringing shame to the family. We were taught not to take shortcuts. I feel blessed that God has given me talent, and I want to get the best out of it without compromising my ethics. (And I personally think the World Anti-Doping Agency's two-year ban for an athlete is too lenient for a first drug offense; I think it should be a lifetime ban.)

Sometimes your eyes and mind can do a better job of detecting cheaters than the tests do. At the 2005 world track & field championships, Rashid Ramzi, a Moroccan competing for Bahrain, not only won both the 800 and 1,500 meters for the first time in meet history, he won them dominantly. He made the world championships look like some high school league meet. When a runner who comes out of nowhere is suddenly dominating the best guys in the world, something's odd. I told some U.S. teammates that I thought the guy had to be using something. Of course, that was just my opinion. Whether or not he was using at that time, we don't know. We do know this: 15 months after Ramzi won the 1,500 at the 2008 Beijing Olympics, his blood sample from that race tested positive in a retroactive test for CERA, a souped-up form of EPO, and he was stripped of his medal.[6] That was not a surprise to many in the sport.

In 2004 Ryan Shay and I did some training runs with Eddy Hellebuyck, who was over 40 years old and was practically leaving us in the dust. It didn't make sense to me. Hellebuyck finished eighth in the marathon trials at age 43 that year, but wound up losing the placement because he had tested positive for EPO in an out-of-competition test before the trials.[7]

Out-of-competition testing is necessary, but it can be a nuisance. Just ask an Olympian. The Olympic sports in general and track in particular have much more comprehensive testing than professional sports in the United States. I have to account for my whereabouts 24 hours a day, seven days a week, 365 days a year so the World Anti-Doping Agency (WADA) and the U.S. Anti-Doping Agency (USADA) can conduct out-of-competition tests, referred to jokingly as "knock and pee." The testers knock and you have to provide an instant urine specimen. No player in Major League Baseball, the National Football League, or the National Basketball Association has such stringent demands to provide information on their whereabouts.

If I change travel plans suddenly—a common occurrence for someone with home bases in both Mammoth Lakes and

San Diego and with three young children—I must inform
WADA and USADA. If testers from either agency show up
and I'm not around, I will be charged with a missed test. Three
missed tests in 18 months would be a violation that could gain
me a two-year suspension.

I've had two misses. One happened when we left San Diego
for Mammoth Lakes a day earlier than we had planned and
I forgot to register the itinerary change with the drug testing agencies. Sure enough the testers came looking for me
that day in San Diego and eventually reached me by phone in
Mammoth. They told me I could comply with the protocol if
I drove to the closest tester in Reno. I was informed that she
couldn't drive to Mammoth because she didn't have a babysitter for her kids. My response: "I need a babysitter too. I
just drove seven hours from San Diego to Mammoth; I'm not
driving another three to Reno." So that was a strike.

The testers always seem to come at awkward times. Once I
was about to leave on a trip to Eritrea when the knock came.
Testers have followed me to church and doctor's offices.
When I retire from the sport, there will be two things I won't
miss—ice baths and out-of-competition testing. But both are
necessary.

///////////////////

Good coaching is also necessary. For 17 years, I've had Bob
Larsen's help. We're a good combination because he's calm and
I'm driven. When I was at UCLA and such a workaholic in
academics, he'd tell me, "Take a deep breath. Don't be in such
a rush. I know you want to do things right. Pause. We don't
think clearly unless we're calm."

He also listened to my body. If I told him, "This hurts," he'd say, "Okay, back off." I had a little trouble communicating with him early on because I wasn't used to discussing things with adults. In my culture, I was used to listening to elders, but not talking much to them. But Coach Larsen was always asking how I felt. He wanted my input on how I was reacting to workouts. He helped me get in touch with my body.

I consider my time with Coach Larsen an internship. I've written down his philosophy. I keep detailed workout diaries that include every workout I've done with him. In the last 10 years or so we haven't had the daily face-to-face contact we did in my UCLA days. Yet Coach got to my hard workout days even when his wife, Sue, was battling cancer and he had to make tough late-night drives from Los Angeles or San Diego, where they had homes. He always wanted his eyes on me for the tough stuff. If we were doing 60-second quarters, he wanted to see if I was straining or relaxed.

BOB LARSEN: We're both pretty meticulous in keeping records, but Meb's even more detailed than I am. Occasionally you can overcoach someone and make the athlete too dependent on you. I wanted Meb to feel that he could make decisions, and I wanted him paying attention to his body. He's a very structured person, but you can get yourself into trouble by thinking that once something is on paper, it has to be done. Workouts should be flexible. Now I can't remember the number of times I'd be thinking about changing something and we'd get on the phone and he'd suggest the very thing I'd just been thinking.

It also helps to have a good agent. I started out as my own agent, getting help from Pete Petersons in entering European track races. When I first turned pro, I talked to two of the bigger agents in the business, Mark Wetmore and Ray Flynn. But they weren't interested when I said I wanted to handle the negotiations for my shoe contract—after all, I was a UCLA graduate with a specialization in business. For a while I was affiliated with Jos Hermens of the Netherlands, whose clients include Ethiopian great Haile Gebrselassie.

After winning the silver medal in Athens, I decided that changing agents might be beneficial. I wanted someone based in the United States who could help me with road races here and get me more involved with marathons. I wanted to market myself in the States and needed help. I talked with Leigh Steinberg, best known for representing high profile NFL quarterbacks, who was dressed in a T-shirt and shorts during our visit. I signed with his firm but left a few months later. I reconsidered Ray Flynn and proposed that he hire my brother Merhawi. Flynn's Tennessee-based firm, whose clients include Ryan Hall and Deena Kastor, had no West Coast representative. I also thought Merhawi could help bring him UCLA athletes and promising Eritrean runners. But the idea didn't fly.

I then asked Merhawi, a second-year law student, if he would be interested in being my agent. He had gone to law school with the intent of becoming an agent, but with an original goal to concentrate on the basketball industry. He wasn't sure if he was experienced enough to become my agent.

I hired Merhawi in early 2005 under one condition: he had to finish his final year of law school at UCLA. Many people

MERHAWI KEFLEZIGHI: I was passionate about Meb, who was going through a transition. I said, "Let me help you navigate this and review some contracts." The more I did, the more I realized, *Hey, I can do this.* I woke up one night and wrote a page-and-a-half proposal. I just wanted to be considered. I realized I really wanted the job and didn't want any regrets down the line that I hadn't pursued it harder.

thought I was keeping it in the family. Trust me: he earned it. Most agents out there don't have a law degree.

In early 2005, I was part of a TV commercial that aired nationally. Through Nike I appeared in an ad for Finish Line stores that turned track into a NASCAR race in which I edged Dathan Ritzenhein at the finish line and had champagne poured over my head. That appearance was part of my Nike contract and didn't earn me any extra money, but it was great exposure.

I did another commercial for MasterCard, which was engineered by Merhawi and Don Franken's World Class Sports, a marketing agency based in Los Angeles that Merhawi had commissioned to pursue marketing opportunities. This one paid six figures. It was clever. I used a "tap and go" cash card at different venues to purchase a drink, a magazine, a ticket to a matinee, and a box of candy and still had time to win a road race. The ad first aired during the 2006 Super Bowl pre-game show and also was shown during 2008 and 2009. I'm still getting residual payments. In 2010 the ad aired in Italy, which is where, in 1986, I saw television for the first time. Who would have thought then that I'd ever be making commercials nationally and internationally?

I'm lucky to have Merhawi. Not only does he hustle to find opportunities for me, he provides all kinds of logistical support—driving me to and from airports, transporting cars from San Diego to Mammoth, helping with the kids—that no other agent would be willing or able to do. It also helps to have complete trust in my agent. Merhawi's company, HAWI Sports Management, now represents seven clients.

The running business can be lucrative for a select few—there are probably just a half-dozen American marathoners making a decent salary—but it also can be cutthroat. If you win a major race like the Boston or New York marathons, you can make well into six figures. But if you have a poor race—even if it's due to illness or injury rather than complacency—your payments can be drastically reduced. You're only as good as your last race.

Many shoe and race contracts contain reduction clauses that can be activated to reduce your salary if you don't reach certain performance goals. One of my contracts had a provision that if I failed to finish in the top four at major marathons, my base salary could be reduced by as much as 30 percent.

I negotiated for that provision to be relaxed. I told them, "If I'm in the top four of a major marathon late in the race, do you want me protecting fourth place or do you want me going for the win?" You can hit the wall quickly in a marathon. In my debut in New York in 2002, I was in the top four after 20 miles, went for the win, and wound up ninth. I missed my contractual cutoff time by 35 seconds, cutting my appearance fee in half. I went for the win, and it cost me money, but I fulfilled my race and life strategy, Run to Win.

There was a time earlier in my career when I spent too much

time thinking about money. I'd write down what certain times would mean in bonus payments and stress about things. Finally I realized I had to get back to basics. I fell in love with the sport because I love the feeling of running and the excitement of competing. And, as my mother always reminds me, my job is to prepare as best I can and leave the rest to God.

At least most distance runners have some advantages compared to shot putters, pole vaulters, or other field event athletes because of our versatility. I have won national championships on the track, road, and cross country. And the road-racing season is year-round. In addition to shorter road races, I can fit in two major marathons a year.

For most collegiate distance runners with professional goals, the first years out of college can be a rough transition. Few runners sign contracts sufficiently large to be able to run full time. All the others have to find jobs with enough flexibility that they can train around them.

The Mammoth Track Club is trying to fill a void in creating opportunities for promising runners. I call Mammoth Lakes a distance runner's heaven because of the altitude, varying terrain, and beautiful scenery. It's a great place to live and train. The club now has about 15 members; all but me are coached by Terrence Mahon. Deena Kastor, the bronze medalist in the women's marathon at the 2004 Olympics, and I are the senior members. The other Olympians are Ryan Hall, Jen Rhines (Terrence's wife), and Anna (Willard) Pierce.

The club gets funding from the New York Road Runners, the USATF Foundation, other sponsors, and the town of Mammoth Lakes. It's great being part of a group, even if we don't all do the same workout. Meeting in the mornings for runs and later for gym sessions makes the work easier and gives the day structure. There's a free exchange of training ideas. Even though Terrence doesn't coach me, he works on my body and is an invaluable source of information for injury problems. We're all about positive energy and encouraging one another.

The group started in 2001 when coaches Bob Larsen and Joe Vigil arranged for runner Philip Price and me to go to Mammoth for three weeks in April. My 10,000-meter American record, set after that stint in Mammoth, focused some attention on our group. We grew in numbers and began to spend more time there. Now there are several groups nationally— the Alberto Salazar and Jerry Schumacher–coached Nike athletes in Portland, Oregon; the Oregon Track Club in Eugene; and the Hansons-Brooks Distance Project in Rochester Hills, Michigan, among them. To continue improving, this is what U.S. distance running needs, clusters of good runners around the country. I'm proud we were pioneers in this.

The more competition, the better. I know this from personal experience, going back to high school. As a professional, I would not have accomplished all I have done without the presence of Alan Culpepper and Abdi Abdirahman. We took turns beating one another in college and for U.S. titles. We pushed each other to become better. Best of all, it was a friendly rivalry. We liked and cared for one another. I enjoyed the runs we'd take together before or after a competition.

It takes a village to raise a runner.

RUNNER'S TIP

Remember, the 22 hours after your workout are important too. Seek active recovery through methods such as icing your legs and stretching. Work on strengthening body parts such as feet and ankles to help prevent injury. Get plenty of rest.

OVERCOMER'S TIP

Start out with reasonable expectations. What you want to accomplish and where you are in the process may be far apart right now. Your assignment is to close the gap.

9.0 / TRIALS AND TRIBULATIONS: A TEST OF FAITH

FOR U.S. MARATHONERS the route to the 2008 Beijing Olympics started in 2007. The U.S. trials that determined the team were held unusually early. The race was November 3, 2007, the day before the ING New York City Marathon.

While my focus in 2007 was to finish in the top three in New York, Coach Larsen and I thought participating in a spring marathon would be a good idea. We targeted the London Marathon in April, as did my training partner Ryan Hall, who was showing promise at longer distances and wanted to experiment at 26.2 miles.

Hall and I were on a similar schedule for the early part of 2007. Our first tune-up was the Houston Half Marathon in January. Ryan hit one out of the park, becoming the first American to break one hour at the distance, finishing in 59:43. I was third in 1:02:22. Nobody was going to beat Ryan that day. He ran away from everyone early. By 10K (6.2 miles) he had a 58-second lead on me.

Two months later, at the Gate River Run, a 15K road race in Jacksonville, Florida, I turned the tables, winning in 43:40, my sixth win in the race. Ryan was second in 44:01. But my win came with a price—a golf ball–sized blister on my left foot.

At first I thought it was just a nuisance. A couple of days later, however, while at home in Mammoth Lakes, the pain became excruciating. I had to get to the hospital, but my car battery had died. I called Deena Kastor, who had won the women's division in Jacksonville, for a lift. When she came to pick me up, I had to use a broom as a crutch to get to her car. "What happened?" she said. "You just won a race two days ago at 4:30 pace and now you can't walk?"

The blister was drained, but there was no great relief. Therapists wound up removing it, leaving a half-inch gash on the bottom of my foot. Six weeks before a major marathon, and I couldn't run. Not a good situation. For three weeks all I could do was cycle, using a Dr. Scholl's donut pad to protect the area, and wait for the skin to grow back and the hole to fill in. Once I could start running, I supplemented my workouts with cycling. Coach Larsen and I decided to give London a shot because I had been in such good shape beforehand.

I wound up dropping out at about 16 miles. My right Achilles had begun hurting after compensating for the altered left foot mechanics as a result of the blister. It's not easy to drop out in London. The volunteers urge you to keep going. I was still in the top 20 at this point. They almost push you back on the course if you're not bleeding. One guy offered to stretch my Achilles. I also had heard that race director David Bedford, who set the world record in the 10,000 in the 1970s, disliked dropouts. But I knew that forcing the issue on a bad Achilles could jeopardize my chances of running the trials in November or even ruin my career. So for the third time ever, I dropped out of a race. (My first DNF [Did Not Finish] was at the 2005 world track & field championships when I ruptured a quadriceps muscle.)

I was feeling pretty low when I boarded a London Underground train for a ride back to the hotel. I was sitting with my head down when we picked up another passenger. I couldn't believe my eyes: it was Haile Gebrselassie of Ethiopia, my hero and maybe the greatest distance runner ever. Suddenly I didn't feel so bad. "What happened?" I asked as Haile came up to me.

"My chest; I couldn't breathe. What happened to you?" I told him my Achilles story.

As we were talking, Stefano Baldini of Italy, who beat me in Athens, got on board. Now I was feeling even less bad than before. "What happened?" I asked. "Hamstring," he answered.

The three of us got off the Tube, and on our way to the hotel we bumped into another dropout, Khalid Khannouchi of the United States, a two-time world record holder in the event and a former London champ. Khalid had Achilles problems too. Now I really didn't feel bad at all. I was in incredible company. Despite all four of us dropping out of the race, there were eight sub-2:09 finishers in the race. This goes to show just how deep the London Marathon field is.

While I was having a tough day, Ryan made a smashing debut. He finished seventh in 2:08:24, the fastest debut ever by an American. He had become a strong contender for an Olympic berth in his new event.

///////////////////

After London, I went to Eritrea as planned with Yordanos and 14-month-old Sara. Since none of our relatives living in Eritrea had been able to attend our wedding, this was an opportunity for Yordanos and me to meet one another's extended families. On my last visit, I had been able to explore my family's roots; this time, I was able to discover hers. I also got to reconnect with some relatives I hadn't been able to see on my first visit. During our stay, I was interviewed for an hour on national TV and featured in a two-page spread in the national newspaper.

I never fail to get inspired on visits to Eritrea. It's great to see relatives, and I love the feeling I get from the people. They don't need a lot of modern conveniences to be happy. They rely on more basic things like face-to-face interaction. Life is simpler than it is in Europe or the States. Not easier, just simpler.

The spirit and self-reliance of the people move me. Here is a country that waged the longest war in modern African history to win its independence from Ethiopia, a country 20 times larger in terms of population and with far superior arms because of backing from the Soviet Union and, at times, the United States. The people are tough; they don't give up. When Bob Larsen was at UCLA, he told legendary Kenyan runner Kip Keino that I had just signed for a scholarship and mentioned I was from Eritrea. "Those Eritreans are fighters," Keino told him.

My father was always telling me that Eritrean soldiers would sometimes have to go three days without food or water. I think about that when I'm going through a tough patch in a marathon, where I have police escorts and water stations every 5K. Then I realize that I don't have it so tough.

Eritrea still has its problems, but I'm proud of some of the strides the country has made in the short time since its independence was recognized internationally in 1993. In the early- to mid-1990s, it had the fastest-growing GDP of any African country. And keep your eye on runners there, such as my friend Zersenay Tadese, a medalist at world and Olympic competitions; Yonas Kifle, a 2:07 marathoner; Yared Asmerom, a 2:08 marathoner (whose agent is my brother, Merhawi); and many others. I'm proud of them just as I'm proud to see the resurgence of U.S. middle-distance and distance running. I get excited seeing runners from both countries doing well.

Once we returned from Eritrea and my foot and Achilles problems were straightened out, training for the trials went virtually without a hiccup. I had a great summer of racing, earning personal bests in all three races. I was fourth at the Bix 7 in Davenport, Iowa, which is a very special race to me. When I first participated in the event in 2002, I immediately hit it off with assistant race director Dan Breidinger and his wife, Mary. Our relationship was so strong that when they adopted an infant daughter, they named her MEB (Molly Elizabeth Breidinger). Anytime I go back to participate in the Bix 7, I stay with the Breidingers.

I also finished fourth at the Beach to Beacon 10K in Cape Elizabeth, Maine, running a rare sub-28 time for an American. Joan Benoit Samuelson is the race's founder. She is a hero, not only in U.S. running, but in women's sports in general. Another unique feature of this race is that runners stay with host families, and Bill and Dena De Sena were my hosts.

I came in second at the Falmouth (Massachusetts) Road Race. The elite athletes in this event are also hosted by local families. My host family is always the Womboldts, who take great care of me. I'd love to see more road race organizers recruit host families.

I hopped over to Europe to run a 10,000 in Brussels, Belgium, finishing in 27:41.26, which got me the Olympic qualifying time for 2008. I had two goals in this race: first, to break the American record; the second and minimal goal was to get the A standard. Fast-paced 10Ks are hard to find, so it was good to achieve at least one of my goals at the Memorial Van Damme meet in Brussels.

Once I got back to full-time training after the racing period, the results continued to be encouraging. I did a 26-miler starting at 7,800 feet, rising to 8,500, and ending at 7,800 in 2:42, faster than I had run before Athens. For the second time, *Runner's World* put me on the cover of their November issue, shirtless. I was leaner and fitter than ever. My summer results indicated I was ready for a marathon PR. Ryan Hall told me shortly before we left for New York, "I hope I'm on the team with you."

I don't take Olympic team berths for granted, even when others consider me a shoo-in. The U.S. system is severe: reputation means nothing; you have to produce on the day. As much as I liked my chances, I figured there were eight other contenders for the three berths: Ryan Hall, Dathan Ritzenhein, Dan Browne, Alan Culpepper, Abdi Abdirahman, Khalid Khannouchi, Brian Sell, and Ryan Shay.

As well as my preparations had gone, there was a last-minute snag. I caught the stomach flu from another runner about 10 days before the trials. All of a sudden, I couldn't keep any food down for several days. We thought about getting IVs, but doctors told Coach Larsen I should have enough time to recover as long as I kept forcing fluids. Coach Larsen was more worried about the situation than I was. He called our fluid replacement blitz "cramming."

I was hoping for the best once I arrived in New York. Because of a wildfire, I had to fly out of San Jose rather than San Diego. Despite the change in plans, I tried to stay relaxed. On the Wednesday before the Saturday race, I had a friendly conversation with Ryan Shay in our hotel lobby. We had been training partners in Mammoth from 2003 to 2005 before he left to train in Flagstaff, Arizona. He had just gotten married to Alicia (Craig) Shay, a top 10,000-meter runner. We talked about training and life in general. Ryan was a fiery, charismatic guy and an incredibly hard worker who was always encouraging. I think he had reached a new level of contentment with his marriage to Alicia. He mentioned that he was considering chiropractic school. His coach, Joe Vigil, who had helped start the elite training group in Mammoth and coached Deena to the bronze medal in the Athens marathon, stopped by. We talked some training before departing.

On the morning of the race, Ryan and I sat next to each other on the bus that took us to the starting line in Midtown. "How cool is this, to own New York City," he said of our police escort. "It's 5:50 in the morning, and the road is open to us." We talked about some international trips we had made. Then we got lost in our music and individual preparations before the race. We hugged before the start.

The course started at Fifth Avenue and 50th Street, continued 1.4 miles in Midtown, and then entered Central Park, where a five-lap circuit ended at the New York City Marathon finish line near Tavern on the Green.

On our second lap, I was at the front of the lead pack when, at about 10 miles, we were nearly cut off by an ambulance on the course. I had no idea what had happened. I looked at Ryan Hall and said, "Let's push it, get it down to three people, and get out of this mess."

He could see my frustration and said, "Isn't it a little too early? Let's see what the next mile is."

It was 4:47. The pace was picking up. I was feeling good— for another two miles, anyway. At about 12 miles, my calves began cramping, and I became worried. Shortly thereafter Ryan Hall began pulling away. He looked great. I realized I had no shot at winning and hoped I could stay in second place. At about 14 miles, Dathan Ritzenhein went past me. I thought, *Protect third place. It's just not your day.*

Then Dan Browne passed me, really moving. "We can catch these guys," he said. I couldn't even respond, I was struggling so much. I was now in fourth, but not for long. Brian Sell was the next to whiz by me. I still had hope, however slim, that I could claim a spot. Maybe Ritzenhein and Browne might also make the team in the 10,000 and elect to do that event rather than the marathon in Beijing.

Next by me was Khannouchi, a native Moroccan who had become a U.S. citizen. Once the best marathoner in the world, he was now fighting injuries. But he was soon past me, leaving me in sixth place with another 5-mile lap to go.

Yordanos was watching the race on television at Tavern on the Green. She knew I was in distress after Khannouchi passed me and I couldn't put up a fight. She called my brother

Fitsum, who was watching along the course, to tell him to tell me to drop out. I never saw Fitsum in the enormous crowd. Dropping out might have been the smart decision. But I didn't consider it seriously because I was not breathing hard. My mind was telling my body to go, but my body would not respond.

The crowd support kept me going. I was in tears hearing comments like, "Meb, you're our hero. We still love you." It hits you in the heart. If I had been running faster, I probably wouldn't have heard them. I was inspired but just couldn't move. The last 1.2 miles took 12:31. I might as well have been walking.

I wound up eighth in 2:15:09. Ryan Hall made winning look easy, finishing in 2:09:02, a trials record. Ritzenhein took second (2:11:06), and Sell (2:11:40), who had led much of the 2004 trials, got third for the final spot. After finishing, I made sure to congratulate all three of them. Good day or bad day, I think sportsmanship is important. They were the best men on the day.

My body was hurting, which I attributed to the hills in Central Park, though they didn't compare to what I had been running in Mammoth. Less than a couple of minutes after I crossed the finish line, a friend who used to run with me in San Diego and Mammoth sought me out. "Did you hear what happened to Ryan?" he said. I assumed he meant Ryan Hall and said that he had run a great race and that I had just talked to him.

"No, Ryan Shay," my friend said. "He died." Shay had suffered a cardiac arrest and collapsed at about the 5.5 mile mark. The ambulance we had encountered on the second lap was the one taking him to Lenox Hill Hospital, where he was pronounced dead. I knew none of this at the time. All I heard was that Ryan Shay had died, and it hit me like a ton of bricks.

I collapsed immediately, crying hysterically. I was shaking uncontrollably on the ground. I was angry at the loss of a wonderful person. I had been depleted physically and mentally in the late stages of the race. Now I was depleted emotionally. I was carried into the medical tent, crying nonstop.

The next thing I knew, I was at a press conference for the top finishers. I was of interest to the media because I was the favorite who hadn't made the team. We had been instructed by race officials not to divulge the news of Ryan Shay's death, to talk only about the race. It was a surreal experience. The news of the death had filtered to the media, though, and there were questions about it. Finally, Mary Wittenberg, the CEO of the organizing New York Road Runners, who had knocked themselves out to make the event a logistical and promotional success, made the announcement about Ryan Shay's death.

We all had a lesson in perspective. Failing to make the Olympic team didn't seem like such a calamity. I was overcome with grief about Ryan's death. But I also was starting to realize there was something seriously wrong with my body. John de Csepel, a general surgeon in New York who had become a friend, practically carried me to a taxi and then into the hotel. I asked my brother and agent, Merhawi, to check on Alicia, Ryan Shay's wife, but she had already left the hotel.

When Josh Cox, another marathoner who is part of the Mammoth Track Club, called me later that day, we talked first about our races. Talking about Ryan was just too difficult. Then I told him I couldn't believe our friend was gone. I choked up, not knowing what else to say. After several moments of silence between us, I finally said, "I don't understand, but I know God is in control." I wasn't trying to be super-spiritual; I just knew that holding on to the reality of God's power and goodness was all we could do in that moment. As Josh said later, "Sometimes knowing God is in control and that He has His perfect plan is our only comfort."[8]

I spent the next three days in a hotel room with Yordanos, forced to crawl on my hands and knees whenever I needed to move. When you can run 4:30 per mile in long races, but it takes you five minutes to get from the bed to the bathroom, something is wrong. Even turning over in bed was an ordeal.

A day or so after the race, when I was still relegated to lying on the sofa in the hotel room, Yordanos said to me, "Honey, give it up. This is America. We have opportunities. You have a degree from UCLA. I have a degree from South Florida. This is not a way to earn money."

She might have had a point. Still, as bad as I felt physically, I thought there was something left in the tank. My workouts and races had been great. I knew what my body could do. I didn't think my ability could have suddenly vanished. I felt I had not yet maximized my God-given ability. I was convinced I could run faster at the marathon, half marathon, and 10,000. "Why don't we pray about it?" I said. "If it's God's will that I can no longer run, that's fine."

During that dark time, we clung to Jeremiah 29:11: "'For I know the plans I have for you,' says the LORD. 'They are plans for good and not for disaster, to give you a future and a hope.'" And so we prayed, knowing that God had taken away my ability to run right then but confident that He could give it back.

As we had planned, we went to Tampa to be with Yordanos's family after the trials, but my legs were swollen and walking was a challenge. As much as I wanted to attend Ryan Shay's funeral, I couldn't.

We spent about six weeks in Tampa before returning to San Diego. I hadn't run a step since the trials although twice a week I received massage therapy from Michael Eggleston. It was my longest voluntary break from running since I started. My legs were feeling better, so I decided to resume running. But something felt out of whack. It seemed as if my hips and belly button were turned to the right when I ran. I felt like a car that needed a front-end alignment. During the Christmas holidays I told my brothers that I was at a critical juncture, that my body seemed to be betraying me and that my running career might be over.

In my search for a solution, I eventually consulted more than 50 doctors, both MDs and chiropractors. I had deep tissue work done on my legs. I visited physical therapists and biomechanical experts. A doctor in Los Angeles thought I had a tear in my rectus abdominus stomach muscle and recommended surgery.

In early January 2008, I called Steve Van Camp (who, remember, is a cardiologist) about the possibility of surgery. I had always valued his advice but, fortunately, hadn't needed his medical expertise before. He put me in touch with Dr. Lewis Maharam, a New York–based sports medicine expert who specialized in treating running problems. I first visited him in Phoenix, where he was the medical director for the Rock 'n' Roll Arizona Marathon.

It didn't take him long to rule out the prior diagnosis:

"I know sports hernias, and you don't have one." He thought I might have piriformis syndrome, a problem high in the hamstring that might require a cortisone injection. But he needed me to get to his New York office for a more comprehensive evaluation.

When I got there in late January, the first MRI scan taken of the hip area revealed no problems. Dr. Maharam conferred with the radiologist, and they started taking additional scans to give them different angles and more information. Their searching paid off.

Dr. Maharam gave me the bad news/good news report. The bad news was that I had a stress fracture on the right side of my pelvis. The good news was that the crack appeared to be healing and that I didn't have to worry about any piriformis problems. He wanted to make me orthotics—customized insoles that can correct foot problems and other skeletal abnormalities—and wanted me back in a month for MRIs to check the pelvic healing.

The stress fracture—which Dr. Maharam described as "like a crack in a hardboiled egg"—probably occurred at the Olympic trials. Structural abnormalities combined with my high mileage had led to a weakening of the area. Dr. Maharam used an analogy to explain the cause: it's like scratching corduroy pants—the more you scratch them, the more likely you are to make a hole. In my view what punched the hole was probably my altered mechanics at the trials from cramping calves that stemmed from the stomach virus. The crux of the problem was that I had run too many miles with my body out of alignment. The idea behind the orthotics was that they would correct my biomechanical problems.

I resumed running, but again, it just didn't feel right. I got discouraging news in February. The MRIs showed the bone was not healing at the expected rate. Coach Larsen and I contacted a doctor I had known from my college days, Aurelia Nattiv. While at UCLA, I had participated in a bone study she was conducting on swimmers and distance runners. Her verdict on my current situation was jarring: because of low bone density, I was on my way to osteoporosis and a narrowing spine. She put me on a crash course of Vitamin D and gave me a prescription for Actonel, a drug that slows bone loss while increasing bone mass and is most commonly used by women and senior citizens.

I had one big question for Dr. Nattiv: Could I run again? I didn't mean competing and winning at the world-class level. I meant simply running. I was immensely relieved when she said yes, that she had a patient in a similar situation who had returned to competitive running at UCLA.

But running was out for the moment. I had to avoid weight-bearing exercise. My new training ground became The Plunge, San Diego's largest heated indoor pool, in Mission Beach. I was there every day, sometimes for up to two and a half hours, for deep-water running. I started to smell like chlorine. Unlike some runners, I didn't use any flotation device during water workouts to help me maintain running posture; I wanted to work harder to stay upright. I'd simulate in the water what my workouts would have been on land. I did intervals and long sessions.

My new training partners were senior citizens taking exercise classes in the water. We encouraged one another. One of them used to tell me, "You make us old folks feel young." We got to know one another. They were excited when Yordanos gave birth to our second daughter, Fiyori, which means "beautiful flower" in Tigrinya, in March 2008. It was a welcome and joyous event amidst a slew of bad news, and it gave me a boost. The seniors told me, "You're lucky. The girls will take care of you in old age." Coach Larsen had a beach house nearby and would often drop by the pool as well.

BOB LARSEN: Running in the water day after day is the most boring thing for runners. It's tough. Meb is the best that I've ever seen at it. I've never seen anyone that dedicated to putting the effort in. He's always been good about the stretching, form drills, and cooldowns. This has saved his career, being able to do the cross-training and hard work in the gym. I always tell doctors and trainers to be careful of what they tell Meb to do. He'll do it to a T and then try to do more.

I resumed running May 9 with hopes of competing at the Olympic track & field trials in Eugene, Oregon, to earn a berth in the 10,000 on July 4. That wasn't much time, especially considering my first run was just 30 minutes. But I had a workout shortly before going to Eugene that gave me optimism. I did a five-mile tempo in 23:32 at 7,000 feet, an average of 4:42 per mile with a heart rate average of 158 beats per minute. I thought I might have a shot at winning; I thought a top-three finish for a Beijing berth was very possible.

We made a family trip out of the 2008 Olympic trials in Eugene, Oregon, also known as Track Town USA. Jim Jaqua, the son of the original lawyer for Nike, and his wife, Mary, opened their and their neighbors' homes to my extended family. Team Meb took over almost a block of Eugene, just a few minutes' walk from Hayward Field on the University of Oregon campus. Jim took me up to a special suite in the Bowerman Building and introduced me to Phil Knight, the cofounder of Nike. My family arrived ahead of time and enjoyed the track meet and festivities with the Jaquas, particularly Jim's daughter, Amber; her husband, Shad; and their two daughters, Tatum and Lauren, a perfect match to our young family.

But my energy wasn't there when it came time to race. I finished 13th (28:39.02) in a race won by Abdi Abdirahman (27:41.89). There was one reason I didn't drop out. Coach Larsen's wife, Sue, had died a couple of days earlier after an ongoing bout with cancer. Whenever I had attended functions at their home with the rest of the UCLA team, I had been struck by her kindness. Somehow, some way, Coach Larsen made it to Eugene for the race, just as he had commuted to Mammoth from his homes in Los Angeles and San Diego during her illness. He had demonstrated great commitment to me during a difficult time, and I wasn't about to dishonor him by not finishing.

In the warm-down area afterwards, we hugged and cried. Some people thought my tears came from not making the Olympic team, but I'm not a guy who cries over something like that. Many things in life are more important than the Olympics. I felt sympathy for Coach Larsen. He had lost his partner of many decades.

As rough a stretch as I was encountering with running, I was getting just as battered in other matters. Besides the loss of

Ryan Shay and Sue Larsen, three Eritrean friends of our family had been murdered in Oakland in 2006 on Thanksgiving Day just before I was to visit them. Then my good friend Mike Long of Elite Racing died unexpectedly in the summer of 2007. My father had gone through some health problems. My annual income had been reduced significantly because of reduction clauses, lower appearance fees, and less prize money.

Left and right I seemed to be getting hit by life's punches. In February 2005 our family had acquired a grocery store in San Diego called Rainbow Supermarket. It was the next step in our American dream—our own business. I put a lot of my savings into it, as did other siblings. Aklilu put his heart and soul into the venture. The whole family pitched in to clean up and renovate the store we bought. When you own a business, there's no vacation. There were times when I was training that I thought I should be in San Diego helping with the store.

The dream turned into a nightmare. In 2007 the store was burglarized in the middle of the night. The thieves not only broke through the ceiling and took the safe—using one of our dollies to remove it—but they came back the next day for more money. Aklilu fought one of them until a robber drew a weapon on him and his fiancée, Mamet. Additionally, my brother Bemnet, my cousin Yoseph, and several other employees were present. That was the beginning of the end of the business. We could deal with some of the financial challenges in the business and the time it required, but we could not deal with putting our lives in jeopardy. To live in a safe land is why we had left Eritrea to begin with.

In retrospect, there were too many obstacles to Rainbow

Supermarket's success. We didn't have experience in the business and made some poor decisions. It was located in a tough neighborhood that didn't attract much outside traffic, and there were chain-store competitors nearby that could offer better prices.

Getting rid of the store became an ordeal. Twice we provided loans to buyers who defaulted. We ended up losing a lot of money—a *lot* of money. My mother and father kept telling us, "Money comes and money goes. Family stays forever." The family could have split over this, the strain was so great on our resources. It tested our resolve. I kept reminding myself of the importance of faith, which was about all we had after the monetary loss from the store and my reduced income from running. At about this time, my dad was in a car accident, just another reminder of how vulnerable we all are. Faith was a frequent topic in my journal during that time, as this entry from February 2008 shows:

> I am going through a rough time of getting healthy, but the Lord is still in control. It's not only injury but sickness, contract reduction, Rainbow stuff, and dad's car accident. We as a family are getting tested quite a bit. I hope and pray the best is still waiting.
>
> I am lucky to have a supportive wife, family, a beautiful (and disciplined) daughter with another one on the way. Life is bright; it just seems difficult at times.

After the Olympic track trials, I felt good enough to enter some road races in the States and track races in Europe. I ran great at the Falmouth Road Race, taking second in my best time there, but I struggled in a 10,000 meters in Brussels after a decent 5,000 tune-up race. I got lapped in the 10,000; Yordanos was watching on the computer at home and later told me the commentators were brutal on me, saying it looked like I was finished as a top runner.

Something was still wrong in those post-trials races. I wasn't able to summon late-race speed as I normally could. My hips felt tight and the pain returned, though an MRI was negative. I seemed to have lost power in my legs.

Terrence Mahon, head coach of the Mammoth Track Club who was knowledgeable about physical therapy and injury treatments, suggested I visit some experts in Toronto. I was considering doing so when Krista Austin, an exercise physiologist I had met in 1999 while living at the Olympic Training Center

---

BOB LARSEN: There were a lot of blows for Meb when you add it all up. Here's someone who was running as well as ever till he got sick 10 days or so before the trials marathon. That took him out of it when he had his heart set on the gold medal. The second blow is he comes back, tries to get in shape, realizes something is wrong, that it's pretty serious, and it's going to take quite a bit of time and effort to overcome.

If you're guaranteed a gold medal, sure, you'd go through all of that. But there's no guarantee with this thing. You're doing it all on blind faith that you're still going to come out okay. You've got to have a lot of faith in yourself and the people you're working with that you can get back to that level again.

in Chula Vista, visited me in Mammoth. When she explained some of the diagnostic tools available at the Olympic Training Center in Colorado Springs, I agreed with her that going there was worth a try. Coach Larsen thought so as well.

Thanks to Krista, I got a high-tech makeover. The Olympic Training Center pulled out all the stops. I got hooked up to all kinds of thermal imaging machines and wires. I was filmed running with a camera that shot 500 frames per second. Biomechanical expert Bill Sands discovered that my left tensor fasciae latae, a hip flexor muscle, was not functioning correctly because it was compensating for weaknesses in surrounding muscles. To rectify that problem, strength coach Bo Sandoval designed a progressive strength program for my core and hips. "You'll feel 25 again," he told me.

For much of late September through late November, we went from 7:00 a.m. to 7:30 p.m. with rehab. There were morning stretch sessions with Krista concentrating on my hips; morning runs and post-run stretching; and finally Active Release Technique—a combination of stretching, massage, and acupressure. There were strength and conditioning sessions in addition to some afternoon runs and more stretching. To promote recovery, I used NormaTec MVP pants, which cyclists have popularized and which utilize computer-directed pneumatic contractions to improve circulation in the legs.

As if Krista wasn't doing enough for my body, she also let me stay at her home. She gave a boost to my morale by inviting Yordanos, Sara, and Fiyori to keep me company for a time. Coach Larsen also visited to check on my progress, which was significant. The same techniques that revealed my problems showed that my form and muscle strength were improving.

That summer, before beginning the therapy in Colorado Springs, I had committed to the 2008 New York City Marathon, but I decided not to run. Although I thought I was getting in good shape—I did a 20-miler at altitude in Colorado Springs in 1:52—I wanted more time to make sure I was ready. In addition, a poor race in New York could further reduce my endorsements. I kept rehabbing until I left Colorado Springs just before Thanksgiving.

If I went back to the New York City Marathon to race, I wanted to be sure I had a chance of winning.

RUNNER'S TIP

If you're injured and can't run, there are still ways to gain fitness. Hop on a bike or exercycle. Go to the pool and do deep-water running. Such workouts can also help an injury-free runner stay healthy longer.

OVERCOMER'S TIP

When situations blindside you, count on God to see you through. You can't imagine the intricate details He will put into place.

10.0 / KING OF NEW YORK

AFTER THE EMPTY running year of 2008—no Olympics, no marathons—I made a commitment to beat as many Olympians as I could in 2009. It was going to be my Olympic year, and the New York City Marathon was going to be my Beijing.

Thanks to a diagnosis of my injuries, significant help from therapists, and a couple of months of rehabilitation at the U.S. Olympic Training Center in Colorado Springs, I was healthy and ready to deliver on my resolution for the new year.

I was feeling so positive that, in January, I sent Mary Wittenberg, the race director of the New York City Marathon, a text: "This is the year." She knew what I meant. Never mind that we hadn't even begun negotiations about my appearance— that wouldn't be finalized until July—I was already thinking about winning the race.

First, I had to test myself in competition again. I began at the Houston Half Marathon, which included Dathan Ritzenhein, who was ninth and the top U.S. finisher at the Beijing Olympics marathon. Ever since seeing him win the bronze medal at the 2001 World Junior Cross Country Championships, I've been convinced he is a special runner. I put in a couple of fast early miles, including a 4:16, and was able to break away after about three miles. At one point I looked to be an easy winner, but around mile eight, my hamstrings started tightening and I had to back off. I found out later that, while riding on the press truck, Dathan's then-coach, Brad Hudson, had bet someone $10 that Dathan was going to catch me. I was thinking, *Just get to the finish line.*

Despite my slower pace, Coach Hudson lost the bet. I crossed the tape in 1:01:25, a personal best and 10 seconds ahead of Ritz. Brian Sell, who also ran the Beijing marathon, was fifth (1:02:36).

My first race in seven months and my first healthy race in more than a year had gone well. I had wanted to show sponsors and others that I was still competitive. Though I thought I was, it was gratifying to have the confirmation in results. Houston was a big turnaround for me emotionally. My good friend Eric Polanski, with whom I frequently exchanged ideas about competitions, was there to cheer me on.

Coach Larsen and I then debated about whether or not I should enter the U.S. cross country championships, which I had not run since 2003. I did a 10-mile tempo run at Miramar Lake in San Diego in 47:32, one second off my personal best for that course. At 33, I felt young again—just as Bo Sandoval had predicted while working with me at the training center in Colorado Springs.

So I entered the championships, in part for contract reasons.

I had been hoping to be selected by USA Track & Field to be part of the five-man team for the marathon at the world track & field championships in August in Berlin. (For the world championships marathon, USATF selects a team rather than holding a trials race, as it does for the Olympics.) But USATF officials could not guarantee me a spot until the qualifying period was over in April. If they had put me on the team, I would not have run a spring marathon. But when they delayed, I thought, *I've got mouths to feed*, and I decided to do cross country and also negotiate with London about running the marathon in April.

I needed a victory at the 12K cross country championships near Rockville, Maryland, in February. I got it by taking control early, widening the lead, and holding off Tim Nelson at the end. The victory was important for a number of reasons. It kept my confidence and momentum going, and it relieved a major pressure. By winning the title, I had fulfilled a contractual point that meant there would be no reduction to my base salary, no matter what happened in any marathons the rest of the year. That victory guaranteed my contract could not be reduced. It allowed me to run freely in marathons. I didn't have to worry about finishing in the top four at London or New York. I felt unshackled. I could concentrate on just running—and winning.

///////////////

I decided to run London, though the negotiation was an adventure. I asked race director David Bedford for a little extra time to decide whether I'd enter. When Merhawi relayed the request on my behalf, Bedford said, "Let me make the decision easy for you: I'm removing the offer." This was uncharacteristic of Bedford, who had always been fair and frank with me. There must have been some type of misunderstanding. Bedford later admitted that "he believed that our request for more time was part of a strategy to get him to increase the offer he had made. He had seen this strategy used before."

Though the offer had been a fraction of what I'd received in the past, it was 100 percent better than the offer from the Boston Marathon. Actually, money had nothing to do with my hesitation. The fact is, Coach Larsen and I were still trying to figure out a smart plan for the year. One option had me skipping a spring marathon altogether to focus on my running fast on the track. Though internally I was convinced that running London was part of a sound strategy for my comeback, I wanted to pray about it a bit longer. To me, it's important to seek God's will before making any major decision.

At first, I was angry with Bedford. Then I recognized that approach wouldn't be productive, and we ended up working out a deal for the same amount. During those discussions Bedford mentioned he didn't think I would ever break 2:08. I mentally file statements like that.

I needed a good marathon because my two previous efforts had been disastrous. In April 2007, I had dropped out of London due to a sore Achilles. In November 2007, at the Olympic trials, I had finished but encountered grief, disappointment, and injury.

Bedford had assembled another incredible field for London in 2009. The leaders had rabbits to provide a 2:04 pace. I went with the second group. Supposedly we were going to be led out at a 2:07 pace, but we went much faster. The first miles were something like 4:38, 4:42, and 4:44. I wound up ninth in 2:09:21 in a race won by 2008 Olympic champ Samuel Wanjiru of Kenya in 2:05:10. My time was a personal best by 32 seconds. Though I had hoped for a sub-2:08, I was pleased with my performance because problems with my anterior tibialis—the shin muscle—had prevented my training from being ideal. I didn't hit a home run, but it was close. And my string of bad marathons was over.

(Ritzenhein finished 11th in 2:10:00, a personal best by 67 seconds. He had hoped for a major breakthrough, though. He wound up leaving Brad Hudson and Eugene, Oregon, and joined Alberto Salazar's group in Portland. Later that summer he finished sixth in the 10,000 at the world championships and set a U.S. record in the 5,000 of 12:56.27.)

Following London, I took the usual post-marathon break with my wife and our two daughters in Tampa so we could visit with Yordanos's family. I wanted to keep things rolling when we returned home and started focusing on the track. I hoped to qualify for the world championships in the 10,000, which meant finishing in the top three at the USA Championships in Eugene. For whatever reason, I have never run well in Eugene. It goes back to my sophomore year at UCLA when I overthought the NCAA 5,000 final and ran poorly. It bothers me that I've never run well in the city known as Track Town USA; it's a mecca for distance running. Distance guys want to run well there just like basketball players want to play well at Madison Square Garden. Maybe I'll try the Eugene marathon one day.

I wound up sixth (28:35.49) in the 10,000. The qualifiers, in order, were Galen Rupp (27:52.53), Ritzenhein (27:58.59), and Tim Nelson (28:01.34). I was disappointed I wasn't going to the world championships, but I felt good about the improvement of U.S. distance running. I remembered the days when you didn't have to break 28 minutes to win a title.

Now it was time to hit the road race circuit. In July I won the Bix 7 road race in Davenport, Iowa, which served as the USATF 7-mile championship, covering the distance in 32:25. I ran the second mile, which is downhill, in 4:08, making me think that those 4:50 miles in marathons would feel easier with that kind of speed in reserve. The win earned me a car, but because it wasn't four-wheel drive and wasn't appropriate for driving in the snow of Mammoth, I took the cash option instead.

I was feeling good enough that I considered going to Europe to get in a fast 10,000 so I could break 27 minutes, a longtime goal. Yordanos and I discussed it a lot. She kept probing, asking me the reason I wanted to do it; I already had the American record. Was it ego? Was it to prove critics wrong? Would it improve my marathon marketability? What was my overall focus? It was like having a second Coach Larsen, who stressed focusing on the ultimate goal when deciding inter-mediate steps. Preparing for New York was the goal, so Europe became a no go.

I drew up a workout schedule from August to the race day in November. This wasn't guesswork; this was based on what I called my 17-year internship under Coach Larsen. I have come across a lot of coaches in my life, and I always try to learn from people. It never hurts. In the process, you learn what to do and what not to do. I put a lot of thought into it, particularly because I want to coach someday.

I handed Coach the sheets detailing my three-month plan. He made two changes. He lowered the elevation for one work-out because of snow at Lake Mary, and he changed a repeat day of a 2K, mile, 1.2K, 1K, 800 meter, mile to a 6 x 1 mile. When I saw that he'd made only minor tweaks, I felt as if I had submitted my graduate thesis and the professor had given me an A.

When I got to the Falmouth Road Race in August, I considered not competing because I had caught a cold and lost my voice. Every time I swallowed, my throat burned. I decided to run anyway, and though I finished fifth (32:12 for seven miles), I was one second faster than when I finished second in 2007.

Once I got my voice back and started feeling well again, I did a 12-mile tempo run in 59-flat at 7,000 feet on a hilly course in Mammoth. Obviously I was strong. Coach Larsen and I thought one more prep race would be good for New York, so I ran the San Jose Half Marathon in early October. I had hopes of breaking one hour. The organizers brought in a pacesetter, but he lasted for only two miles. I needed more pace-setting help than that in order to crack one hour, and I lost pace. But I was headed toward victory and a personal best, and as I neared the finish line, I saw on the overhead clock that I had a chance to break 1:01. Not the milestone I originally wanted, but a milestone nonetheless. I was so focused on the final sprint that I didn't see the four people holding the finish tape. Head down in concentration, I crossed the finish line but off to the side of the tape. Still, 1:01-flat was another personal best, by 25 seconds.

What made the summer of racing more impressive was that it occurred while we were remodeling the kitchen of our house in Mammoth Lakes after it had been damaged by a water leak. For about three months, from June through August, our routine was disrupted. Friends were telling me, "You're running PRs while remodeling? That's incredible." We had to spend a lot of time outside the home to avoid the dust and commotion of the construction. Yordanos, pregnant with our third child, Sara, Fiyori, and I were regulars at local parks. After runs, I'd ice my legs in a creek. Often I'd read the *Prayer of Jabez* with Fiyori, who would be nearby. Afterward we'd throw a blanket down on the ground and take a nap. We had some enjoyable family time that summer, but we were glad when the kitchen was completed.

Obviously I was fit. I was hoping I had benefited from all the lessons I had learned in my previous four New York City Marathons starting when I made my debut there in 2002. That race I discovered the price the body pays for getting carried away by the screaming crowds on First Avenue and running too fast too early in the race.

I thought I could have had a couple of wins in New York with the right breaks. In 2004, 70 days after winning the silver medal in Athens, I finished second to South Africa's Hendrick Ramaala, who had dropped out in Athens and was a late entry in New York. The crucial gap occurred late in the race when I grabbed my bottle at the mile 24 fluid station. I was more focused on Timothy Cherigat, who was coming off a win in the Boston Marathon, than Ramaala, who was better known as a half-marathon specialist at that point.

While Cherigat and I were drinking, Ramaala bolted ahead, putting maybe 40 meters on us. I wasn't too concerned; I still thought Cherigat was the bigger threat. Once he began falling back, I took off after Ramaala but could not eat into his lead. He won in 2:09:28, 25 seconds faster than me. The difference in first and second place amounted to $110,000 in prize money, not counting sizeable bonuses. Even by New York prices, that was a lot to pay for a drink. Ramaala has run more than 30 marathons, and, other than the 2004 Mumbai Marathon, that remains his lone win. He was better on that day. Ramaala has proved himself to be a marathoner, not just a half marathoner, and he has become a good friend.

The day after the 2004 race, I accompanied Hendrick and women's winner Paula Radcliffe of Britain to the *Late Show With David Letterman*. I'm a fan of the show and was hoping to meet the host. I also was hoping I might be introduced as the top American in the race, though I didn't get time with Dave or mention on the show. *Maybe if I win this thing one of these days,* I thought.

In the 2005 New York City Marathon, I finished third (2:09:56) when Paul Tergat (2:09:30) beat Ramaala by one second for the win. I was coming off a ruptured quadriceps (front thigh) muscle that forced me to drop out of the 10,000 at the world track and field championships. I had minimal training entering the race—eight weeks with none over 100 miles. When Ramaala made one of his trademark surges on First Avenue, he ran a 4:22 mile. I ran that same mile in 4:23—the fastest mile I had run since the ruptured quad in Helsinki at the world championships that summer. I hung with Tergat and Ramaala until the end, when my lack of overall mileage was exposed. Afterward Coach Larsen told me, "If we can just get you to stay healthy and train, you can win this thing."

I thought 2006 might be the year. I felt ready despite a hamstring cramp during a half-marathon tune-up. The first bad omen was lost luggage—on a direct flight—that contained my favorite racing shoes. Usually I put my shoes and running uniform in a carry-on, but not that time.

There was more trouble after we went to dinner on Thursday before the Sunday race. I had chicken fettuccini and wound up with food poisoning. No one else in our party of eight got sick; I was the chosen one.

During the race my gastrointestinal problems continued, and I had to make several pit stops. It was the year that legendary cyclist Lance Armstrong was running, creating a lot of speculation about how his aerobic capacity would translate to the marathon. Every time I went into a portable toilet along the course, I was thinking, *I hope Lance doesn't pass me.* He didn't, but I wound up 20th in 2:22:02, my worst time ever in the marathon. Then I heard that Marilson Gomes dos Santos of Brazil had won in 2:09:58, a time I surpassed on the New York City course in 2004 and 2005, with less than ideal preparation. Had I been healthy, that should have been an easy time for me to run. It could have been my race, but it wasn't. Marilson won on the day.

Now, for the 40th New York City Marathon in 2009, I felt more than ready. After waking up on September 20, I told Yordanos that I had dreamed that I had won New York. "Believe in God and anything is possible," she said.

Then she asked if I was interested in the results of the Great North Run, a half marathon in England that included NYC Marathon contenders and had been run earlier that Sunday. She broke it to me gently that Martin Lel of Kenya had run 59:32 and Jaouad Gharib of Morocco, 1:00:04. Their times were a lot faster than my best for the distance. "I guess you can forget about that dream then," I said as a joke. I waited several seconds, digesting all the information, before adding, "They still have to show up on November 1. They have to win on the day. Those guys may have peaked too soon." I then prayed that I could get to the starting line healthy. I thought if that could happen, the rest would take care of itself.

Before arriving in New York for the race, Yordanos and I watched replays of my previous marathons there. Yordanos had come a long way from our first meeting, when she didn't know the difference between a tempo run and a negative split. She commented that she thought I could have won a couple of titles if I had done more following than leading in the early stages. "You do too much of the work. Don't do so much leading," she told me. I had my orders.

Once race time drew near, we took every precaution at home to minimize Murphy's Law—what can go wrong, will— which had struck in the past. We asked Sara's preschool teacher, Rena Davis, to inform us if kids in the class were sick. We'd rather have Sara stay home than pick up a bug at school and transmit it to me. Though it contradicted family tradition, we even kept her out of school as a precaution for a couple of days just before the race. (Hey, it's preschool; she'll be able to make it up.)

When Fiyori came down with the sniffles, I called Mammoth friend and runner Brian Ball and crashed with him for a couple of nights. Once I got to New York, I got my body worked on more than usual before a big race. The treatments included massage, active-isolated stretching, chiropractic adjustments, Active Release Technique, and Tecar, an Italian therapy using ultrasound that Mario Scerri introduced to me following my quad injury in 2005 (an injury originally misdiagnosed as a cramp).

I was constantly using hand sanitizer to avoid germs and hoped nothing would go wrong before or during the race.

Before the event, which also was serving as the U.S. championships, I wasn't mentioned prominently. The international runners included late entrant Robert Cheruiyot of Kenya, who had won Boston four times and Chicago once; Kenya's James Kwambai, the number three marathoner of all time, who was coming off a 2:04:27 in May in Rotterdam; Hendrick Ramaala, who got the 2004 NYC title at my expense; Morocco's Jaouad Gharib, a two-time world champion and the 2008 Beijing Olympics silver medalist; and Brazil's Marilson Gomes dos Santos, a two-time NYC winner. Martin Lel, a two-time NYC and three-time London champion coming off the notable Great North Run win, had withdrawn because of injury.

The U.S. field was impressive with Ryan Hall, the 2007 Olympic trials champion; old buddy Abdi Abdirahman, who had turned his track speed into a 2:08:56 marathon; and Jorge Torres, who had run the 10,000 at the Beijing Games and was making his debut at 26.2 miles.

I was the 10th fastest runner in the field. David Monti, the race's elite athlete coordinator, termed me a "long shot" in an e-mail to Merhawi. I filed that away. I was confident about my chances. The day before the race I went up to 90th Street and Central Park West to do my usual marathon eve routine. I did an easy three miles, six to eight 100-meter strides at slightly better than race pace—on the cinder bridle path and not the asphalt, to give my legs a break—and a half-mile cooldown. I did the run with Dr. Andrew Rosen, who was part of my recovery effort in 2008. When Bob Larsen and I took a cab back to the hotel, he told me I looked great and figured I was in better shape than Cheruiyot, who was a mystery man due to his late entry.

BOB LARSEN: Sometimes the guy who comes in late is in great shape; sometimes he's not quite sure where he is. I'm not clairvoyant, but I had a feeling Meb was going to have a great race, which means a high finish but not necessarily winning. He was ready; I was letting him know he had the green light. We always want to be somewhat conservative with the expenditure of energy early, but I wanted him to know that he should be thinking about challenging everybody in the race. I had a feeling it might come down to him and Robert.

/////////////

The New York City Marathon starts on the Verrazano-Narrows Bridge, which contains the biggest hill on the course. (The biggest hills are on the bridges.) As a result, everyone typically starts slowly and eases into the race. That's the way I like it. As the race started, I was mindful of Yordanos's admonitions not to do any challenging in the early going. I stayed in the front row of a large pack that was close behind a couple of early leaders. (Since 2007 New York has been run without rabbits, unlike some major marathons such as London, Chicago, and Berlin.) I didn't want to get tripped or bumped by being in the middle of a large pack. I wanted to run freely. To use a running expression, I wanted to "fall asleep" for as long as I could. I wanted to get to Central Park, at about the 24-mile mark, as relaxed and rested as possible—something that hadn't happened in my four previous NYC marathons.

I couldn't put myself on cruise control, though, because of Morocco's Abderrahime Bouramdane, who made a number of mini moves ahead of the pack before drifting back. Ryan Hall told me not to worry about him, that he was a rabbit for countryman Jaouad Gharib, whom I greatly respected. It turned out that assessment of Bouramdane was wrong.

Bouramdane hit the halfway point, on the Pulaski Bridge, which connects Brooklyn and Queens, in 1:05:07, four seconds ahead of a pack of about a dozen runners. By the time we were past the 15-mile mark and on the Queensboro Bridge, we had dropped two-time champ dos Santos. Along with me, three Americans were in the lead pack—Hall, Abdirahman, and Torres. Two things struck me. All the lead runners were altitude trained. And the pack was an indication of how U.S. distance running was improving. In 2001, the last time New York had served as the U.S. championship, Scott Larson had won it by finishing 13th overall in 2:15:26. I realized that simply winning the U.S. title was going to be tough in this race.

I was also thinking about what was coming up. The Queensboro Bridge, also known as the 59th Street Bridge, leads into Manhattan at mile 16 with raucous crowds along First Avenue. It's where a lot of rookies—and I was one of them once—can get carried away. Ramaala has made some ridiculously fast miles between 16 and 19 his signature.

It almost happened again. This time I noticed Ramaala trying to recruit others—Bouramdane, Kwambai, and Kenya's Jackson Kipkoech—to help him. That was a sign he wasn't feeling strong enough to break the pack by himself. That group made some mini surges. I wanted to stay within four or five seconds of them to keep an eye on them. Looking around the lead pack I saw the veterans, Cheruiyot and Gharib, staying calm. Gharib is a tactician; he makes his moves count. Cheruiyot didn't win Boston and Chicago by doing crazy things. You stay with the key guys.

Even though the pace was sane, with miles just under 5 minutes, the pack was thinning. This is what I mean by the course making moves for you—the distance takes a toll; the race demands patience. Hall, Abdirahman, and Torres were dropping back after mile 17, and so was Gharib. I wanted to make sure the pack didn't slow; I wanted to put Gharib away. If he were feeling good, he'd have been up front with us. I wanted to start reducing the pack, just like I had done in Athens.

Four of us—me, Cheruiyot, Bouramdane, and Kwambai—were out front by mile 21 after we had crossed the Willis Avenue and Madison Avenue bridges into the Bronx and back into Manhattan. I was excited to be the top American, but I didn't want to be satisfied with that. I felt relief that we were bearing down on Central Park and that I was feeling strong. I thought it was going to come down to a sprint finish, just as I had visualized in training runs. I tucked behind the other guys to conserve energy. I figured the course was going to be making another move soon.

I assessed the lead pack. Bouramdane had made a lot of surges, which can sap a runner. I saw Cheruiyot and Kwambai talking and thought they might be hatching a plan. I was ready to cover any moves. Before we hit 22 with a 4:56 mile, however, Kwambai and then Bouramdane began fading. That left me and Cheruiyot.

We made an odd couple. At 6 foot 2 inches, tall for a marathoner, Cheruiyot had about eight inches on me. Good thing we weren't playing basketball one-on-one. At times I'd tuck behind him, letting his bigger frame break the wind for me. Then I'd pull up next to him on his right just to make my presence felt. When we came to a late-mile water station, I grabbed my bottle but observed him before taking a drink. I wasn't about to get burned again, like in 2004, by a late-race drink. Cheruiyot took a quick sip, and I took a slightly longer one, eyeing him the entire time.

The entrance to Central Park at Fifth Avenue and 90th Street, known as Engineers Gate, is one of the few areas I know well in the big city. I'm comfortable there. I had done strides there the day before. I've run through the spot many times in Central Park races and training runs. As we entered the park, having just run a 4:56 mile, I made a slight surge, creating a gap between us. If Cheruiyot had been feeling good, he'd have covered it, so I expanded my lead. As I did, I prayed, "Okay, Lord, I initiated the move. Now please help me get to the finish line first."

As I was pulling away in the park, I passed the spot where Ryan Shay had collapsed before dying in the 2007 Olympic trials marathon. I had logged thousands of miles with him and still missed my friend. While passing a bench that had been installed there in Ryan's memory, I thought, *May he rest in peace.* Remembering Ryan inspired me to summon my reserves as I headed toward the finish.

In visualizing the New York race during my training runs, I had been thinking of doubles. I wanted a U.S. win and a New York win. I wanted a title for myself and a title for Ryan Shay.

I wanted attention for San Diego and Mammoth. I wanted glory for the USA and for Eritrea. And now, with less than two miles to go, it looked like it was going to happen.

At times I was fixated on the race, thinking mechanics, mechanics, mechanics. I wanted my shoulders down and back, my stride crisp, my body tall. Other times I was having nothing but career flashbacks. It was similar to Athens, where all my running acquaintances and experiences passed through my mind. And there was a new dimension this time. I was also thinking of all the doubters and all the slights I had received.

I was expanding the lead running along Central Park South and heading toward Columbus Circle, where the crowds were thick and loud. The noise was deafening and pushed me toward the finish. I heard shouts of "USA! USA!" and "Go Meb!" It was the thrill of a lifetime. Turning right and back into Central Park, I had a 34-second lead with 385 yards left.

I popped my USA singlet a couple of times. I flashed double thumbs-up and waved to the crowd. I was trying to take in the moment. I was also thinking, *Rein yourself in. Don't celebrate too much. Get to the finish.* I was about to win my first marathon. I was about to become the first American winner in New York in 27 years. I had believed all along I could do it. But I couldn't believe it was actually happening. All those close calls. All those unlucky breaks and weird injuries. Food poisoning. Stress fractures. Ruptured quads. All kinds of problems at the wrong times. The countless hours of rehab and cross-training.

Then there were all those people who thought I was over the hill. All those who said I'd never win a major marathon. But this was more than proving them wrong. This was about getting the most out of myself, about seeing my Run to Win philosophy in action. I thanked God for listening to my prayers. I had thought He might be taking my career away two years before. Now He had given me victory. This win was my way of saying thanks to Him and to all those people close to me who had provided help and encouragement at many low points.

The ups and the downs of our family ran through my mind. I recalled the passing of my grandfather Aboy Berhe Mehanzel; Ryan Shay; Sue Larsen; Mike Long; our family friends in Oakland; the priest who married Yordanos and me; Mussie Mehari, a good family friend from Boston; my friend Mussia's father, Baba Teklemariam; my good friend Adam Jacobs, founder of TheFinalSprint.com; Phillip Rangel III, whom I had met at a running camp and become good friends with; and John Jaqua, Nike's former lawyer and a family friend. God had called some special people to heaven.

The tears were welling up. I was overwhelmed with emotion. At least I didn't miss breaking the finish line tape as I had in San Jose. Once through the tape, which was being held by Governor David Paterson and Mayor Michael Bloomberg, I thanked God and then did a push-up. Actually I was trying to kiss the ground but remembered how Stefano Baldini had cramped so badly while sitting down after winning the Athens Olympics, so I popped up quickly before any muscles could spasm.

I saw Yordanos, seven months pregnant, holding Sara and Fiyori. I saw my mother. We all were crying. My father was there, the guy who told me I could beat the world at the 2000 Olympics. I had told him it would take time to do that. It had taken nine years, but I had finally beaten the world in New

York. I had almost beaten the world in Athens, but no family was there to celebrate my silver medal. Here I had my parents, wife, and daughters. There was deep, deep joy.

Mary Wittenberg handed me an American flag. I arranged it right side up before holding it aloft and draping it around my shoulders. I had no such moment in Athens, so I was going to be sure to get it right here. I jogged back onto the course, exchanging waves, high fives, and comments with fans—the victory lap I didn't get in Athens.

I saw Cheruiyot and embraced him. I told him, "You're a great champion. You've had great days in Boston. This was my day today." Ryan Hall and I hugged. As disappointed as he was in finishing fourth, I could tell he was genuinely happy for me. He will have his days in the future. He is too talented and too committed not to.

During my euphoric post-race wandering, we took a picture. I am standing with Yordanos and the girls, my parents, Coach Larsen, and Merhawi—my brother, agent, and close friend. What a moment. I was with special people after a special accomplishment. Yordanos nailed it when she said, "It's a miracle of God's work." Two years after the worst day of my running career—losing Ryan Shay and suffering a bad injury at the 2007 Olympic trials in New York—I was on top of the world in Central Park.

I had run a personal best of 2:09:15, an average of 4:56 per mile. Not bad for a 34-year-old on a tough course. Cheruiyot was 41 seconds back; Gharib came in third in 2:10:25. Hall was fourth in 2:10:36; Bouramdane was fifth (2:12:14); and Ramaala sixth (2:12:31). What added to my gratification was the fact that four other U.S. runners placed in the top 10—Torres was seventh (2:13:00); Nick Arciniaga, eighth (2:13:46); Abdirahman, ninth (2:14:00); and Jason Lehmkuhle, tenth (2:14:39). The United States hadn't had six in the top 10 in New York since 1979, when Bill Rodgers won the last of his four New York titles.

The payday was a good one too. The prize money came to $170,000. I won't get into specifics, but the bonuses from the race and sponsors exceeded the prize money. Even though I was ecstatic after the race, I maintained my usual discipline. I got stretched out by good friend and constant supporter Jimmy Lynch and then took an ice bath in the hotel.

////////////////////

The feel-good moments were interrupted a few days later when CNBC sports business reporter Darren Rovell made critical comments about my win in an article on the Internet. He suggested it wasn't really a victory for the United States, since I had been born in Eritrea and was a naturalized citizen. Rovell compared me to "a ringer who you hire to work a couple hours at your office so that you can win the executive softball league."[9]

Readers responded almost immediately by writing impassioned comments in my defense. A media firestorm erupted as well. It was heartening to me to feel such support. Obviously, Rovell wasn't familiar with my story, but it was getting old, this business of whether I was really an American or American enough. Two of America's greatest marathoners were born out of the country. Frank Shorter was born in Germany to American parents. Alberto Salazar was born in Cuba. Neither of them had to defend their citizenship.

Drowned in a sea of criticism, Rovell issued an apology. It read, in part, "It turns out, Keflezighi moved to the United States in time to develop at every level in America. . . . That makes a difference and makes him different from the 'ringer' I accused him of being. Meb didn't deserve that comparison and I apologize for that."[10]

I accept the apology. I forgive though I struggle to forget. For just a moment I wanted to sue the guy. Then I thought he might be a good coauthor for the autobiography I wanted to write. It might have given him the opportunity to really get to know me and my story. I didn't act on either idea.

Fortunately, I have memories of other, more enjoyable experiences after the race. I finally appeared on the *Late Show With David Letterman*. Dave asked me a couple of questions as I stood on the set to his right, dressed in a gray Nike sweatsuit with my gold medal hanging from my neck. I cracked Dave up when he asked me what I was doing in the last mile. "Celebrating," I said. I didn't realize he was asking for my split time in the final mile.

I even got to announce that night's Top Ten List: "The Top Ten Thoughts That Go through Your Mind While Running the New York City Marathon":

10. "Wow. Staten Island is even more beautiful than I imagined!"

9. "Cool. Mapquest found a route that's only five miles."

8. "Am I experiencing a runner's high or is it the bus fumes?"

7. "Is that the finish line or crime scene tape?"

6. "Why can I run the 26 miles in less time than it takes to play a World Series game?"

5. "Car!"

4. "Cramp!"

3. "Who's that little boy waving at me? Oh, it's Mayor Bloomberg."

2. "I forgot to bring the exact change for the Verrazano Bridge!"

1. "I really hope that was Gatorade."[11]

In all, I got about five minutes of air time that ended with a handshake and bouquet of roses. Another dream accomplished.

The Onion, a satirical publication that is distributed on newsstands and online, ran a picture of me riding a horse ahead of the field at the marathon. The accompanying story began as follows:

> Officials from New York Road Runners stripped American Meb Keflezighi of his 2009 ING New York City Marathon victory Wednesday after a blood sample taken from his fetlock was found to contain high levels of performance-enhancing horse. . . . Keflezighi finished the race in 48 minutes and 12 seconds, easily setting a new world record and defeating his nearest competitor by one hour and 20 minutes.[12]

My win brought other perks as well. I attended a New York Knicks game the day after my win and was presented with an official jersey with the number "09" and "Meb" on the back. I got it autographed by one of my favorite players, Chris Paul of the New Orleans Hornets. Between his warm-up shots, I introduced myself to Chris. He said, "I know who you are. I can't believe you did a push-up after finishing the marathon."

I was most moved by the e-mails and text messages I received. Bernard Lagat, a Kenyan turned American and a 1,500/5,000 medalist at the 2009 world championships, said my run was great inspiration as he began his training for the coming season that day; Alberto Salazar, a hero of mine and the last American to win in New York, sent congratulations, saying he was happy for me, my family, and U.S. distance running. One of the senior citizens I had met during my pool workouts wrote that she was thrilled for me. My victory and comeback seemed to be resonating with the big names as well as everyday people. It was very gratifying.

Later in the month, Yordanos, the girls, and I flew first-class to New York for the Macy's Thanksgiving Day Parade. I rode with Miss America on a float that had a replica of the Statue of Liberty. I loved the symbolism. After the parade, we enjoyed Thanksgiving dinner at fellow marathon runner Eileen Patrick's beautiful home.

It was nice to be king of New York, however temporary.

RUNNER'S TIP
Visualize during runs. See yourself accomplishing goals. Put yourself in race situations during training. Throw in surges during a workout and visualize yourself breaking away from competitors or covering their moves.

OVERCOMER'S TIP
Recognize distractions before they detour you. Remain focused and you'll progress.

11.0 / THE BELL LAP

WHEN I WENT TO THE STARTING LINE of the Boston Marathon in April 2010, I thought I had some lucky numbers in my favor. It had been 27 years—just like in New York—since an American (Greg Meyer) had won Boston. And it had been 27 years since an American (Alberto Salazar) had won the New York–Boston double.

I wanted to be a streak buster again. Instead, I finished fifth in 2:09.26 in a race won by Kenya's Robert "the Younger" Cheruiyot in a course record 2:05:52. The time was a shocker. It beat by 1:22 the previous record set by Robert "the Elder" Cheruiyot (no relation), a four-time Boston winner and the runner-up to me in New York in 2009.

I had hoped that either I or my buddy Ryan Hall, who finished fourth (2:08:41), would end the streak of non-American winners in Boston. Despite my disappointment when that didn't happen, my performance there might have been a better example of my Run to Win philosophy than New York.

I summed up that sentiment in a message to my Facebook and Twitter followers the following day: "I gave it all I had yesterday. I Ran To Win. Thanks for all the support."

I had done my best in preparing despite a difficult situation. In late January my training was going at least as well as it had been before New York. Then I fell twice on icy patches—while walking, not running. Both times I landed on my left knee, which became swollen and sore. I had to take off two and a half weeks—cross-training was out because cycling and water running irritated the knee—and drastically reduce my mileage during three other important weeks. I made other adjustments, such as dropping afternoon runs, to get to the starting line healthy. I had only five weeks of 100-plus miles when normally I'd have at least 10 entering a marathon.

I hung with the leaders until we were into the Newton Hills at about 17 miles. Then my left quadriceps muscle started bothering me so much I was reminded of the time I had to drop out of the 10,000 meters at the 2005 world championships with what turned out to be a ruptured quad. I had to back off and let Cheruiyot and the others go. (Dr. Maharam later confirmed that my Boston injury was indeed a longitudinal quad tear.)

For much of the rest of the race, I was in no-man's-land, by myself with no one to draft off or help me along. The vocal Boston crowds kept me going with their shouts of "USA! USA! USA!" and "We love you, Meb!" Once I got through the hills at mile 21, I started having stomach problems.

I did the best I could on the day. In fact, I dug very deeply the last 10 miles, possibly more deeply than I did with the win in New York. I was heartened by many post-race comments. Joan

Benoit Samuelson told me I ran "a gutsy race." Coming from her, that meant a lot. The two-time Boston champion defines courage. She qualified for the 1984 Olympics 17 days after knee surgery and won the first Olympic marathon for women with a bold, early move in those Los Angeles Games.

My 2:09:26 was my fastest time at Boston, surpassing the 2:09:56 I ran there in 2006. And, on a course not known for producing fast times, I had come within 11 seconds of my personal best, despite a less-than-ideal training period.

The race was my sixth sub-2:10, which gave me the lead in that category among Americans. I'm the number eight American of all time and want to make my way up the list. But I'm proud of the consistency my number of sub-2:10s demonstrates.

I believe running is God's gift to me, so I give it my very best in training and competion. Of course, winning a race is special. At those times, as I'm thanking God, it's easy for me to tell Him, "I know this is what You created me to do."

But I also realize that winning doesn't always mean getting first place; it means getting the best out of yourself. One of my greatest joys is inspiring other people to perform at their best. Whenever I'm talking to fans or signing autographs, I encourage them to keep reaching for their goal, whether it's beating a four-hour personal best in a marathon or running to help raise money to fight cancer.

I think exercise, in fact, is one of the best ways for young people to learn goal setting and to become all they can be. In that spirit, after the race I headed to New York City, where I announced the start of my foundation, MEB, which stands for Maintaining Excellent Balance. The idea behind the foundation is to emphasize education, health, and fitness to youth.

I believe that sports is one of the best ways to teach young people the value of determination, hard work, and a balanced approach in every endeavor. Those virtues then transcend the playing field and impact everyday life.

I had been thinking about launching a foundation to promote this idea for years, but getting over the injuries of 2007 and 2008 occupied my time. The win in New York provided a good platform. We're still in the early stages of developing corporate and programmatic partners, but I was pleased when the ING New York City Marathon granted the foundation 20 charity entry spots in the 2010 race, which will help us raise funds. I'd like to be able to put together as good a team for the MEB Foundation as the one I have for my running. We've started by retaining Carnegie Sports and Entertainment in New York to help manage the foundation.

Scott Kasen, a recreational runner trained by my friend Jimmy Lynch, was so impressed by our vision that he pledged $10,000 at our launch held at Foot Locker's RUN store in New York. Dick Johnson, CEO of Foot Locker, who loves running and has entered the Berlin Marathon, spoke at our event. Additionally, NYRR CEO Mary Wittenberg and members of her amazing team attended the event. I was gratified that Frank Sullivan, who is a friend, a marathoner who had just finished Boston himself, and a justice for the Indiana Supreme Court, also attended the announcement.

From New York I went to Washington, D.C., to be part of another launch, the National Physical Activity Plan, an attempt to fight the problems of inactivity and obesity among youth (as well as all other segments of the American population) with fitness initiatives. It's a natural fit with the MEB Foundation.

INDIANA SUPREME COURT JUSTICE FRANK SULLIVAN JR.:
Meb's running embodies his parents' values: unfailing
integrity, powerful ambition, careful planning, personal
sacrifice, tenacious hard work, persistence, and perseverance.
Just as Meb has been inspired by his parents' values, Meb's
values inspire us.

I appeared at briefings in the House of Representatives and
the Senate, telling legislators and staffers that my own running journey started with a mile run in PE class. Who would
have guessed the kid who arrived in San Diego on October 21,
1987, with no knowledge of English would speak to legislators
on Capitol Hill?

So what's next? I would love to keep running competitively for another three years and make the teams for the 2012
London Olympics and 2013 world track & field championships. I know I can run faster in the marathon, half marathon,
and 10K. If those things don't happen, though, so be it. I'll still
be content with my productive and consistent career.

I must admit that I feel a couple of voids. I'd love to win
the Boston Marathon. I haven't won a medal in the world
championships; in fact, I haven't ever run well at the meet.
And I still haven't broken four minutes in the mile, though I
have a 1,500-meter equivalent of 4:00. I guess you can take
the runner out of the mile, but you can't take the mile out of
the runner.

Once I retire from competition, I plan to stay involved in
the running community. I know I'll run for fun. I'd love to
become a motivational speaker and appear at road races and

schools. I love interacting with people. I try never to turn down an autograph request, and I enjoy answering training and nutrition questions.

I will also get into coaching. I have been fascinated by the science and art of workouts for a long time. While in high school I trained a football player, Jeff Stoike, to run 800 meters in 2w:02, which gave both of us a sense of accomplishment. Upon returning from the 2000 Sydney Olympics, I helped Paul Greer, coach at San Diego City College, for one season, before I realized it was taking too much time and energy from my own running. I love drawing up training plans. I've learned from the best, with a 17-year internship under Coach Larsen and seeing Joe Vigil and Terrence Mahon in action. I have also learned some of the physiological aspects of training from Dr. Krista Austin. I have picked up a lot of tips along the way from world-class runners and coaches.

I think I may already have lined up my first athlete. Just recently my family and I went together to the 2010 Fourth of July Footloose Freedom Mile in Mammoth Lakes, where I was the official starter.

As we passed the awards table on our way to the starting line, four-year-old Sara looked up at me and said, "I want a trophy." What a perfect teaching moment. I knelt down in front of my little girl and explained that she would have to *earn* a trophy. That meant committing herself to practicing and then running the race.

"Would you like to run the mile next year?" I asked.

"Yes, Daddy."

Uh-oh, I thought. *What have I just gotten myself into?*

Whether Sara (or either of her sisters) ultimately decides to run competitively is up to her. As our daughters grow, Yordanos and I will ask only that they put forth their best effort in whatever they do.

That's really the message I most want to convey, whether I'm running, coaching, or speaking. I like how the apostle Paul, who used the ancient Isthmian Games as a metaphor for our spiritual life, put it in 1 Corinthians 9:

> *Don't you realize that in a race everyone runs, but only one person gets the prize? So run to win!* (verse 24)

As every marathon runner knows, you must prepare yourself for the journey. Without proper training, you will never finish. And even with proper training, you never know what will happen on race day. The weather, the course conditions, your own body—all may seem to conspire against you.

"If there is no struggle, there is no progress," said the great American abolitionist Frederick Douglass. What an apt description of the marathon. And what a perfect description of life.

> *All athletes are disciplined in their training. They do it to win a prize that will fade away, but we do it for an eternal prize.* (verse 25)

As important as training and fitness are, they are not the top priority. Sports may bring you great joy; they may help support your family; and they can certainly bring glory to the Lord. Yet, as Paul points out, it's even more critical that you and I submit to the daily discipline of obeying God, knowing that He promises to reward us and supply all our needs.

As I often say, whoever has the better day will win the marathon. No runner is victorious every time. You will not always win in life either. Nothing is guaranteed, no matter how hard you've worked. Injuries are part of running; disappointments and setbacks are part of everyday life. But if you keep doing the right things, eventually the results will go your way.

> *So I run with purpose in every step. I am not just shadowboxing. I discipline my body like an athlete, training it to do what it should.* (verses 26-27)

Winning in life doesn't happen when you overcome just one thing—do or die. It's persevering, knowing that difficulties are bumps in the road, not the end of the world. It's continuing to do the right things, knowing your time will come. After all, you have to conduct yourself like a champion before you can ever win a championship.

Whatever you do, then, give it your best. Persevere in overcoming obstacles. When you do, you'll be running to win.

RUNNER'S TIP
Set gradual, realistic goals. Then go after them aggressively. Once you reach the goals, come up with a new set. Keep challenging yourself, and you'll get reinforcement by meeting the standards you've set.

OVERCOMER'S TIP
Expect to succeed if you are committed and persevere.

ACKNOWLEDGMENTS

BY DICK PATRICK

This book was a collaboration of a lot of parties. First of all, thanks to Meb for applying the same work ethic and determination to this project that you do to training and racing. Merhawi, you provided great advice, patience, and context, plus you were a great roomie. Yordanos, your time and ideas were greatly appreciated, as was your enabling of Meb to spend so much time away from the family. Thank you, Russom and Awetash, for the *injera*, *himbasha*, Eritrean dishes, and the attention to detail you gave to the text. Fitsum, your childhood recollections often helped Meb and me connect the dots.

Meb and Merhawi are thankful to Paul Batura, who brought his vision of a book on Meb to Tyndale House Publishers, and to D. J. Snell, whose guidance through the book industry has been priceless. The brothers also have appreciated the team at Tyndale, including Jan Long Harris and Doug Knox, both of whom believed Meb's story was worthy of being published; and Kim Miller, Nancy Clausen, Yolanda Sidney, and Sarah Atkinson, all of whom helped edit, arrange, and promote the book.

The Van Camps were instrumental in enabling this project to be completed. I can't thank Gail and Steve enough for the living quarters, the comprehensive scrapbooks, and the sustenance, both nutritionally and spiritually. I owe a special debt of gratitude to Indiana Supreme Court Justice Frank Sullivan Jr. for his generosity, his research on Eritrea, and his background article on the country.

To Adam Freifeld of NBC, I am also indebted for important help. When others failed, Adam produced video footage of Meb in Athens in 2004 and New York in 2009. Longtime friend and TV stat man Walt Murphy, Bill Bennett of UCLA sports information, stat maven/announcer extraordinaire Scott Davis, and human database Ryan Lamppe of Running USA went out of their way to promptly dig up important information. It was great to have someone as knowledgeable about both distance running and geography in Sean Hartnett to provide information on Russom's journeys out of Eritrea. Bob Larsen has been generous with his time and knowledge through the years; I only wish I could have spent more time with him at his beach house. Eric Peterson also was more than generous and helpful as were two other coaches, Eduardo Ramos and Ron Tabb.

We would not have made deadline without the transcribing heroics of my niece, Alexis Aceves. To brother-in-law Chris and Gina thanks for editorial suggestions, information on San Diego, and your hospitality.

I might not have written this book without the advice that Frank Coffey, Wayne Coffey, and Jim Donovan offered to a rookie writer woefully ignorant of the publishing business. Jeré Longman's encouragement to seek out Meb and suggestions about as-told-to books also were crucial. Jim Dunaway and Jim Memmott have been mentors and patient friends going into a fourth decade.

Thanks to marathon fixtures Mary Wittenberg and Richard

Finn of New York, along with Jack Fleming of Boston. I also appreciate the help and encouragement provided by announcer/distance guru Toni Reavis, who knows the game and the personalities; track beat colleagues Tim Layden of *Sports Illustrated* and Phil Hersch of the *Chicago Tribune*; those Vienna, Virigina, baseball authors Tim Gay and Tim Wendel; author/historian/track nut/longtime friend George Wright; runner/editor/writer Jim O'Brien; longtime friend and editor Ron Roth, who released me from a freelance assignment to complete the book; ex-800 great and current agent Rich Kenah; and PR agent Sara Hunninghake. To Jim and Phil Wharton, I appreciate the help on this book and all the other help through the years. Meb also thanks them and their colleague Jimmy Lynch for his help and friendship.

Thanks to my family for all their support. My sisters, Maria Patrick and Lisa Leet, never failed to be encouraging and upbeat. At home, no one held it against me that I missed Jody's birthday, Eamonn's high school graduation and summer league triple, or the hoop game where Shea sustained a concussion. A village wrote this book.

MEB'S YEAR-BY-YEAR PERSONAL BESTS

AT SAN DIEGO HIGH SCHOOL

Year	1,600m	mile	3,200m
1991	4:22	N/A	9:30.9
1992	4:18	N/A	9:18.79
1993	4:11.82	N/A	9:11.95
1994	4:06.15	4:05.58	8:51.8

AT UCLA

Year	1,500m	5,000m	10,000m
1995	3:47.48	13:52.06	30:41.24
1996	3:45.04	13:37.00	29:55.75
1997	3:43.95	13:33.97	28:26.55
1998	3:42.29	13:26.85	28:16.79

PROFESSIONAL YEARS

Year	5,000m	10,000m	marathon
1999	13:40.86	28:29.27	N/A
2000	13:11.77	27:53.63	N/A
2001	13:23.16	27:13.98	N/A
2002	13:21.87	27:20.15	2:12:35
2003	13:20.50	27:57.59	2:10:03
2004	13:34.00	27:24.10	2:09:53
2005	13:20.71	28:10.57	2:09:56
2006	N/A	28:18.74	2:09:56
2007	N/A	27:41.26	2:15:09
2008	13:33.29	28:28.44	N/A
2009	N/A	N/A	2:09:15
2010	N/A	N/A	2:09:26

MEB'S MARATHON HISTORY

Date	Race	Position	Time
11/3/02	New York City	9th	2:12:35
10/12/03	Chicago	7th	2:10:03
2/7/04	Olympic trials	2nd	2:11:47
8/29/04	Athens Olympics	2nd	2:11:29
11/7/04	New York City	2nd	2:09:53
11/6/05	New York City	3rd	2:09:56
4/17/06	Boston	3rd	2:09:56
11/5/06	New York City	20th	2:22:02
4/22/07	London	Did Not Finish	
11/3/07	Olympic trials	8th	2:15:09
4/26/09	London	9th	2:09:21
11/1/09	New York City	1st	2:09:15
4/19/10	Boston	5th	2:09:26

MEB'S NATIONAL TITLES

Date	Distance/Event	Site	Time
7/14/00	10,000 (Track)	Sacramento	28:03.32
2/18/01	12K Cross Country	Vancouver, WA	34:54
3/10/01	15K (Gate River Run)	Jacksonville	43:14
2/10/02	12K Cross Country	Vancouver, WA	35:45
3/9/02	15K (Gate River Run)	Jacksonville	42:48
6/21/02	10,000 (Track)	Palo Alto, CA	27:41.68
7/20/02	7 Mile (Bix 7)	Davenport, IA	32:36
9/15/02	Downtown 5K	Providence, RI	13:45
3/8/03	15K (Gate River Run)	Jacksonville	43:31
4/5/03	NY Road Runners 8K	New York	22:28
9/1/03	20K	New Haven, CT	58:57
3/13/04	15K (Gate River Run)	Jacksonville	43:19
3/27/04	NY Road Runners 8K	New York	22:16
7/9/04	10,000 (Track)	Sacramento	27:36.49
3/11/06	15K (Gate River Run)	Jacksonville	43:43
3/10/07	15K (Gate River Run)	Jacksonville	43:40
1/18/09	Houston Half Marathon	Houston	1:01:25
2/7/09	12K Cross Country	Derwood, MD	36:06
7/25/09	7 Miles (Bix 7)	Davenport, IA	32:25
11/1/09	NYC Marathon	New York	2:09:15

DISCUSSION QUESTIONS

CHAPTER 1: AN AMERICAN DREAM

1. Meb describes having to hear naysayers predict that he didn't have a chance at winning the NYC marathon in 2009. Share a time when you were in a similar situation. How did you respond to those who doubted you?

2. Meb writes, "I am often at my best when things look the worst." What does he mean? Is this true of you as well? If so, explain.

3. What does the American dream mean to you? What does it take to achieve it?

4. Meb Keflezighi prepares himself thoroughly for every race he enters—hard work that often pays off. But even when he doesn't win, Meb chooses to honor the winner. Are you personally satisfied when you do something well, even when you are not the winner or are not acknowledged in any way? Does that come easy to you or is it something that you struggle with?

5. On the start line of the 2009 ING New York City Marathon, Meb prayed that he would be successful and win. Have you ever prayed for success in some aspect of your life? Is it wrong to do so? Explain. If it doesn't happen, what do you think that tells you about God?

CHAPTER 2: OUT OF ERITREA

1. As a small child, Meb was impacted by the example of his parents' strong faith and reverence toward God. How did this affect Meb's outlook on life? Who helped you understand who God is? What did that person say or do that made God real to you?

2. Meb's parents encouraged Meb and his siblings to pray often. How important is prayer to you? Do you think prayer affects your relationship with God? How so?

3. Two aspects of God that Meb's parents explained to their children are His holiness and power. How would you describe God to someone? Which of His characteristics immediately come to mind? How have you seen those aspects of God in your life?

4. Today, after receiving an Olympic medal and making a name for himself as a top runner, Meb has not forgotten the struggle he and his family faced during his childhood in Eritrea. What aspects of your own past do you cling to today? How did they help shape the person you are?

5. Meb writes that his parents are his heroes and his role models. Their trust in God and devotion to their family inspires him. Who are your heroes? What did they teach you?

6. How might America seem like heaven to Meb, a 12-year-old boy who had lived through poverty and violence in Eritrea?

CHAPTER 3: COMING TO AMERICA

1. The Keflezighi family was a team. Meb remembers Fitsum's top ninth grade student award as "our most rewarding

moment." Discuss the importance of being surrounded by a trusted team of supporters. Who is on your support team?

2. Knowing the advantages that it could provide their children, education was strongly emphasized by Meb's parents. In what way did this serve as preparation for the discipline required to be a marathon runner?

3. Meb's parents instilled a strong work ethic in Meb and his siblings. They said that if you work hard, the rest will follow. Did you have strong role models growing up? What words of wisdom did they give you that you continue to live by today? If you are a parent, what advice do you want to pass on to your children?

4. Because Meb's father, Russom, knew how critical education was for his children, he laid down strict rules about studying. Do you think his approach was too restrictive? Why or why not? What was the hardest work you ever did to achieve a goal? What was the outcome?

5. Meb learned valuable lessons from growing up in a large family—like planning ahead and paying attention to details. Whether you grew up in a large family or not, family dynamics do influence you in many different ways. Can you think of specific things you picked up from your family that are assets to you? Detriments?

6. Dick Lord, Meb's PE teacher, immediately recognized his student's athletic talent, which was later fine-tuned by Coach Eduardo Ramos. Steve and Gail Van Camp befriended high schooler Meb, investing their time to help him reach academic goals. Did you have a teacher or mentor who saw and helped develop your potential? Have you ever let that person know what you are doing now and

how much you appreciate the time and encouragement he or she gave you? Have you yourself been a mentor or have you thought of being a mentor to someone else?

7. Balboa Park's Morley Field is a special place to Meb—he still considers it his "home field" where he nurtured his passion for running. Do you have a place with special memories for you? What happened there that changed your life? Have you ever revisited it? What does returning there mean to you?

8. Though Meb would have loved to run a sub-4 mile, he knew it wasn't his top priority. Explain a situation when you had to examine and prioritize your goals. What was the outcome?

CHAPTER 4: UCLA DAYS: STUDENT FIRST, ATHLETE SECOND

1. UCLA coach Bob Larsen considered Meb a strong long-distance runner prospect based on Meb's performances in high school. When Coach Larsen met Meb's family, what impressed him the most? Even though they were from two completely different cultures, what did the coach and the Keflezighis have in common? Have you ever met someone whom you immediately connected with, only to find out later how similar your stories were? Did that surprise you?

2. What impressed Meb the most about Coach Larsen? Why were they the perfect athlete-coach team? Have you ever found a coach, teacher, or boss who brought the best out in you?

3. Creating a balance between priorities is often a difficult task. As much as he wanted to succeed as a runner, Meb also knew that he had to establish himself academically. What do you believe is the key to achieving this balance?

4. When Meb was not given a UCLA travel bag right away, he was mad at Coach Larsen. Later, Meb realized that Coach was sticking to his principles. Have you ever been in a similar situation, either as the person who feels slighted or as the person enforcing the rules? Were you able to get through it and remain friends? If so, explain.

5. In his sophomore year of college, Meb began second-guessing his choice to attend UCLA. He envied friends in programs at other schools and seriously considered transferring. Have you ever had serious second thoughts about a decision you made? Did someone help you see the wisdom behind that decision?

CHAPTER 5: TURNING PRO AND LIVING SMALL

1. One person Meb admires is the late John Wooden, legendary UCLA basketball coach. Wooden never talked to his teams about winning; instead, he told his players to push themselves to their full potential. Why was that a crucial concept for Meb?

2. In 1998, Meb faced a major decision—what country would he compete for, his native country of Eritrea or the United States, his adopted country? In the end, his decision seemed to be a win-win situation for both countries. Do you think he made the right decision? Have you ever faced a major decision where there were several good choices? What process did you use to help make your final decision? In hindsight, do you regret the decision you made or can you see how it was God's perfect plan?

3. Meb's attitude for the mid-July 2000 Olympic trials was "to remember the hard preparation I had put in, be thankful

I was healthy, and leave the rest to the Lord." How easy is it for you to prepare well and then leave things in God's hands? If you need to work on that attitude, what would help you become stronger?

4. Meb's mother often told him and his siblings, "You have to think ahead and prepare, but ultimately it's God who will finish the job." What "jobs" has God finished in your life? What is He still in the process of completing?

5. Meb writes, "I believe in setting high goals, but I also believe in being realistic. Some people say you can do whatever you want to do, but I don't think that's always right." Do you agree or disagree?

6. At the 2002 ING New York City Marathon, Meb admits that he got his "PhD in the marathon." What did he mean by that? What lessons had he learned for future races? Have you ever earned a "PhD" the hard way, through making and learning from mistakes?

7. After the marathon, Meb visited Eritrea with his mother for the first time since they left. There, his attitude changed about competing in marathons. What changed for him? What had been the catalyst for the change? Has any situation in your life caused your perspective about something to change dramatically? If so, explain.

CHAPTER 6: ATHENS . . . ANOTHER JOYOUS MOMENT

1. Going into the 2004 Olympic track & field trials for the 10,000, Meb admits that three things gave him an edge: having cinched a berth on the team as a marathoner, having a chip on his shoulder, and being in love with Yordanos. How did each of these help his performance?

2. As an ambassador for long distance running, Meb wants to inspire the next generation of runners. Is there something you have always dreamed of doing or are planning to do to inspire young people, either your own or others? How can you help them capture your vision?

3. During a training run on Crete before the Athens Olympics, Meb was attacked by a dog. Have you ever had something totally unexpected catch you off guard that it significantly affected your life? How did you regroup and get back on track?

4. The last two miles of the Olympic marathon, Meb started thinking of all the people who had helped him get to that moment. He writes, "A lot of people got me to the Olympic Games. I felt my victory was for all the people I encountered on my journey." Can you recall an achievement in your life that was only possible because of the host of people who helped you along the way? If so, explain.

5. Just past mile 23, Stefano Baldini from Italy made his move, but Meb let him go. Baldini ended up winning the gold medal. After the race, Meb reflected on his decision. "I decided at that point to protect the medal. I don't think I lost the race as much as Baldini won it." What does this tell you about Meb's decision-making process while competing? What lessons might that have for you?

CHAPTER 7: LOVE STORY

1. Both Coach Larsen and Steve Van Camp gave Meb advice regarding finding his future wife. Whether you are married or single, did you receive relationship advice? What was it? Did you follow the advice? What was the outcome?

2. Almost immediately after meeting her, Meb was convinced that Yordanos was the woman God wanted him to marry. Have you experienced situations—whether it was finding your spouse or another significant event in your life—where you could clearly see God's hand at work? If so, explain.

3. It is an Eritrean custom for children to take on their father's first name as their surname. In your family, do you have any traditions regarding names? How would you answer the question that Shakespeare posed: "What's in a name?"

4. Meb writes, "Without Yordanos, I would be like a car with a flat tire." What did he mean by that? Do you have someone in your life that you could describe in a similar way? What analogy would you make? ("Without _____, I would be like _____.)

CHAPTER 8: LIFE ON THE RUN: THE ELITE GAME

1. At the beginning of his pro career, Meb had a conversation with running superstar Paul Tergat that set Meb on a course to achieve his own acclaim in the running world. What did Tergat say to him? Why did that make a difference in Meb's life? Can you think of any conversations you have had in your life that have impacted you significantly? What changes did they implement?

2. Every elite athlete has a disciplined routine—Meb is no exception. As you read his day-by-day training schedule, did it make you think of areas in your life where you need more discipline? What are they?

3. Meb spends his regular scheduled time with God in an unusual circumstance. What is it? Why does it work so well

for him? Do you spend time with God on a regular basis? Is there a certain time and place that this happens? How does that strengthen your relationship with God?

4. Meb resonates with Jabez's prayer in 1 Chronicles 4:9-10. Why does it mean so much to him? Do you have a verse that resonates with you? Why is it so special?

5. What has been the most effective deterrent for drug use for Meb? Why has it worked so well? What keeps you from doing what everyone else is doing? How difficult is it for you to remain strong?

6. In the earlier part of his career, Meb admits that he "spent too much time thinking about money"—to the point of stressing over things. But then he reexamined why he fell in love with running in the first place. What did he discover? How did that help him? Is there something in your life that you need to get back to basics on, remembering why you loved it in the first place? If so, explain.

CHAPTER 9: TRIALS AND TRIBULATIONS: A TEST OF FAITH

1. At the 2007 London Marathon, Meb had to drop out of the race because of a bad Achilles. Yet in the midst of his disappointment, a series of things raised his spirits. What happened? Have you ever felt sorry for yourself and then been encouraged by some surprises? Were you satisfied with the way the circumstances eventually turned out?

2. Whenever he visits his home country of Eritrea, Meb is moved by the spirit and self-reliance of the people there. How would you describe the people of your home nation? What makes you the most proud?

3. Before the 2008 New York City Marathon, Meb ran into his friend and competitor Ryan Shay. It would be the last time they'd talk—Ryan suffered a cardiac arrest on the course and died. Have you discovered that life is too short? In what way? What do you need to do right now that you shouldn't put off any longer? Whom would you like to connect with?

4. Meb describes 2008 as personally "getting hit by life's punches." Things continued to spiral out of control after Ryan Shay's death, like Meb's severe health issues and the financial hit when the family business failed. Yet again and again, Meb was able to say, "The Lord is in control." Have you ever felt life spinning out of control for you? Were you able to see, in the midst of everything, how God was in control? If so, explain.

CHAPTER 10: KING OF NEW YORK

1. Going into the 2009 running season, Meb exuded confidence. He was certain it would be his comeback year. Have you had a comeback experience in your life? What did you do to bolster your confidence?

2. Before Meb entered the London Marathon, he made it a serious matter of prayer. In fact, Meb always tries to seek God's will before making any major decision. Are you seeking God's will in a major decision you are facing now? If so, explain.

3. What did London Marathon race director David Bedford say to Meb that fired the marathoner up? Have you ever been able to use someone's negative perspective to your advantage, turning it into a positive motivational tool?

4. Meb considers his 17-year association with Coach Larsen as an internship—he's always learning something from his mentor. Who have you "interned" with in your life? What makes that relationship invaluable to you?

5. In September 2009, Meb dreamed that he won the New York City Marathon. Have you ever had an actual dream come true? What surprised you the most?

6. The 2009 New York City Marathon win was gratifying for Meb on many levels. What were they? Discuss an accomplishment in your own life that is especially meaningful.

CHAPTER 11: THE BELL LAP

1. Like 400-meter Olympic medalist Eric Liddell nearly a century before him, Meb knows running is what God "created me to do." Have you discovered God's gift to you? How are you using it? Are there ways to develop or utilize it even more?

2. Meb writes, "You have to conduct yourself like a champion before you can ever win a championship." What does he mean by that statement? What characteristics of a champion do you need to work on in your own life?

3. Now that you've finished the book, what one lesson from Meb's life would you most like to apply to your own?

NOTES

1. Charles E. Cobb Jr., "Eritrea Wins the Peace," *National Geographic*, June 1996, 84.

2. Buster Olney, "Running Now a Refuge," *San Diego Union*, January 29, 1991.

3. Steve Brand, "Cavers' Keflezighi Sets Record," *San Diego Union-Tribune*, November 21, 1993.

4. Steve Brand, "San Diego Preps Win 2 State Titles," *San Diego Union-Tribune*, November 28, 1993.

5. Steve Brand, "Keflezighi, Hauser Qualify," *San Diego Union-Tribune*, December 5, 1993.

6. "Doping Scandal: IOC Strips Bahrain's Ramzi of 1500 Gold," *USA Today*, November 19, 2009.

7. "Sports Briefing: Running: Marathoner Is Suspended," *New York Times*, December 11, 2004.

8. Josh Cox, "Meb's Great Race," *STV* magazine, April 2010, http://www.sharingthevictory.com/vsItemDisplay.lsp?method=display&objectid=A1CF7CD4-C29A-EE7A-E3EB21F59D622BBE.

9. Darren Rovell, "Marathon Headline Win Is Empty," CNBC.com, November 2, 2009, http://www.cnbc.com/id/33587668/Marathon_s_Headline_Win_Is_Empty.

10. Darren Rovell, "What I Got Wrong about Keflezighi," CNBC.com, November 3, 2009, http://www.cnbc.com/id/33603449/.

11. *Late Night Show With David Letterman*, November 2, 2009, © 2009 Worldwide Pants Incorporated. All rights reserved. Used with permission.

12. "New York Marathon Winner Tests Positive for Performance-Enhancing Horse," *The Onion*, November 5, 2009, http://www.theonion.com/articles/new-york-marathon-winner-tests-positive-for-perfor,2845/.

A PORTION OF THE PROCEEDS FROM THE SALE OF THIS BOOK GOES TO

The MEB Foundation

Sports play an integral role in the lives of our young people and teach lessons that transcend into all aspects of life. The MEB Foundation is a leader and collaborator in health, education, and fitness, seeking to align with organizations that share our goals of:

- empowering youth to "Maintain Excellent Balance" in work and play
- inspiring families to lead healthy, active, balanced lives
- providing the tools and resources to learn positive life skills
- engaging children in academics, in and out of school hours
- connecting entire communities through education, health, and fitness

Find out today how you can help The MEB Foundation address some of the most significant needs facing youth in this country and around the world.

For more information, visit Meb Keflezighi's personal Web site, www.marathonmeb.com.

THE MEB
FOUNDATION

GET IN THE GAME WITH TYNDALE HOUSE PUBLISHERS

Quiet Strength
by Tony Dungy

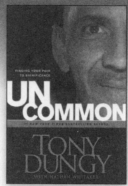

Uncommon
by Tony Dungy

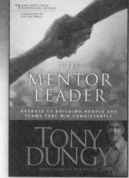

The Mentor Leader
by Tony Dungy

Run to Overcome
by Meb Keflezighi

Coming Back Stronger
by Drew Brees

Game Plan for Life
by Joe Gibbs

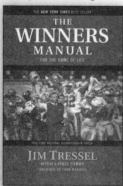

The Winners Manual
by Jim Tressel

Unthinkable
by Scott Rigsby

LT & Me
by Loreane Tomlinson

For more information on our exciting books from some of today's
most popular sports figures, visit www.tyndale.com.

CP0437